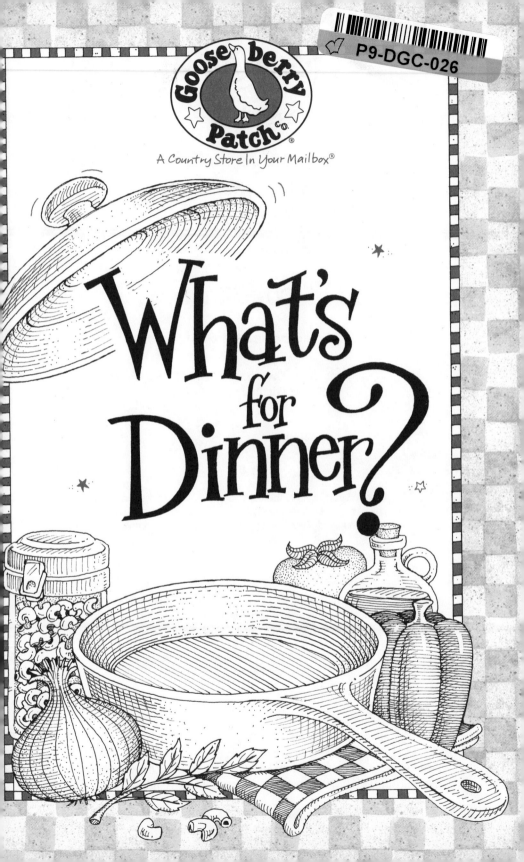

Gooseberry Patch

A Country Store In Your Mailbox®

What's for Dinner?

A Country Store In Your Mailbox®

Gooseberry Patch
600 London Road
P.O. Box 190
Delaware, OH 43015

★

1·800·854·6673

www.gooseberrypatch.com

Copyright 2004, Gooseberry Patch 1-931890-52-8
Second Printing, February, 2005

Do you have a tried & true recipe...

tip, craft or memory that you'd like to see featured in a **Gooseberry Patch** book?
Visit our web site at **www.gooseberrypatch.com**, register and follow the easy
steps to submit your favorite family recipe.
Or send them to us at:

Gooseberry Patch
Attn: Book Dept.
P.O. Box 190
Delaware, OH 43015

Don't forget to include the number of servings your recipe makes, plus your name,
street address, phone number and e-mail address. If we select your recipe, your
name will appear right along with it...and you'll receive a FREE copy of the book!

Contents

Dedication

For our friends who know those 3 little words all too well..."What's for Dinner?"

Appreciation

A special "Thanks" to all who shared their recipes and helped us answer the world's oldest question!

Can't-Miss Casseroles

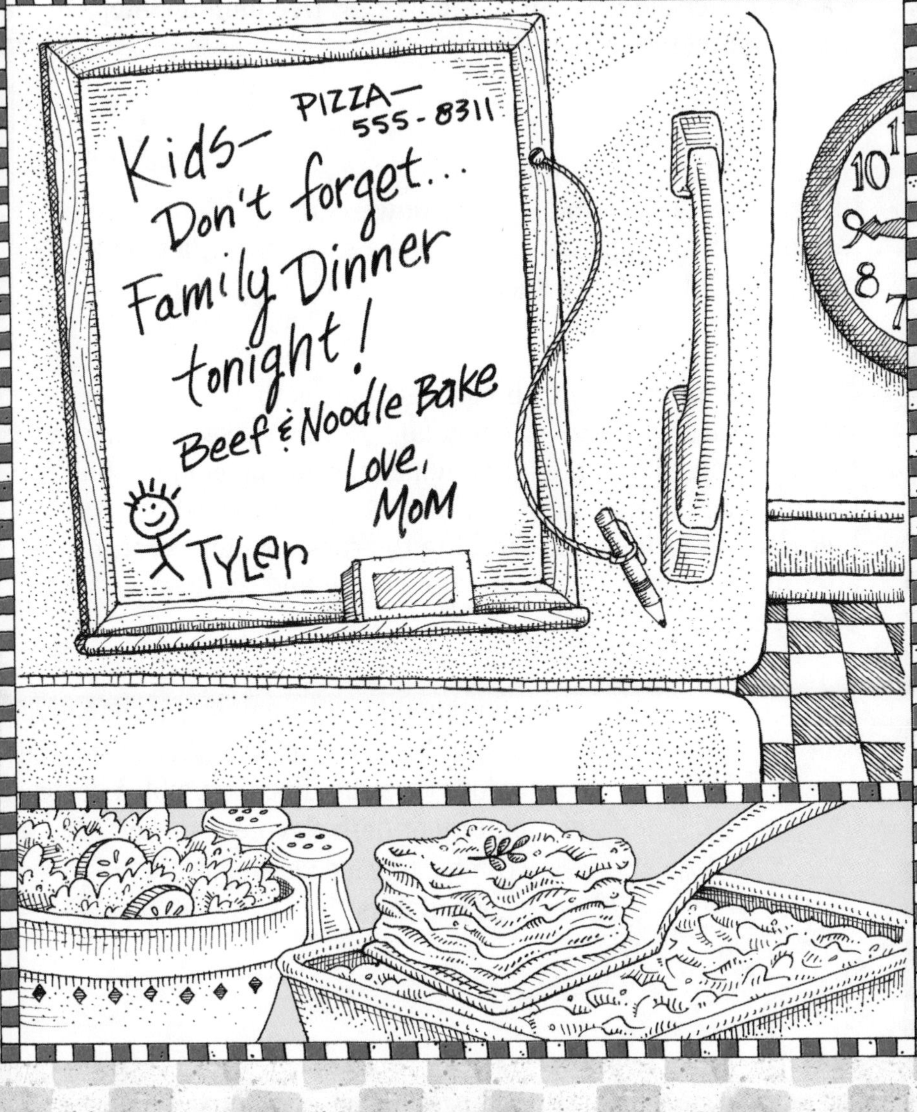

Super ideas for simple suppers!

★ Rinse ground beef with very hot water before cooking...it does wonders to cut fat! Fill a pan with very hot, but not boiling, water and let the meat sit in the pan for five minutes. Repeat, then drain before cooking.

★ Stock up on pre-cut and peeled vegetables like carrots, onions and broccoli flowerets available at the supermarket or at the salad bar...they make casserole preparation a snap.

★ One of the nicest things about casseroles is they're so easy to make ahead and freeze to enjoy later. While casseroles can be frozen unbaked or baked, just remember to allow additional baking time because they're frozen. An instant-read thermometer is ideal for checking the casserole temperature after it's been in the oven one hour. It should reach 160 degrees.

★ Sprinkle on some tasty toppings to give casseroles extra pizazz...French fried onions, bread crumbs, crumbled bacon, buttery or herb-flavored cracker crumbs, toasted pecans or chopped nuts.

Golden Chicken Casserole

Annette Kennon
Auxvasse, MO

A quick and hearty meal my family loves every time I make it.

3 c. cooked chicken, diced
2 10-3/4 oz. cans cream of
   chicken soup
1 c. milk
1 T. chicken bouillon granules

salt and pepper to taste
3 15-oz. cans mixed vegetables,
   drained
8-oz. tube refrigerated crescent
   rolls

Combine all ingredients except crescent rolls in a saucepan; cook over medium heat until heated through. Pour into a greased 13"x9" baking pan; unroll crescents over top of chicken mixture. Bake at 400 degrees for 15 minutes or until crescent rolls are golden. Serves 8 to 10.

An oh-so-simple photo gallery! Coil strands of wire, insert them into salt and pepper shaker holes, then slip favorite photos inside.

Creamy Tuna-Noodle Casserole

Elena Engelsman
Anaheim, CA

A make-ahead microwave casserole that's so simple and delicious...I like to serve it with a crisp salad.

10-3/4 oz. can cream of
   mushroom soup
1 c. milk
6-oz. can tuna, drained

1 c. elbow macaroni, uncooked
1 c. peas
1/2 c. onion, chopped
1 c. shredded Cheddar cheese

Whisk soup and milk together until well blended. Stir in remaining ingredients. Place in a greased 2-quart microwave-safe casserole dish. Cover and refrigerate overnight. When ready to prepare, microwave on high 13 to 15 minutes or until bubbly. Serves 2 to 4.

Pages of laminated sheet music from a yard or garage sale make fun placemats!

Bacon-Spinach Casserole

Sarah Shesko
West Farmington, OH

An easy, cheesy way to get your family to love spinach!

4 slices bacon, cut into bite-size
    pieces
1 onion, chopped
4-oz. pkg. sliced mushrooms
1 c. light whipping cream
1 t. lemon juice

1/2 c. shredded Swiss cheese
1/2 c. shredded provolone
    cheese
1/2 c. grated Parmesan cheese
16-oz. pkg. spinach

Fry bacon in a skillet until crisp. Add onion and mushrooms to skillet; sauté until onion is tender. Add whipping cream, lemon juice and cheeses. Place spinach in a bowl; top with sautéed ingredients and blend well. Place mixture in a well-greased 2-quart casserole dish and bake at 350 degrees for 45 minutes to one hour. Serves 4.

For whimsical placecards, string baby-bracelet beads
onto jewelry wire, available at craft stores. Just punch
holes in a folded card, slip the beaded wire through
the holes and curl the ends.

Beef Lombardi

Elizabeth Quigley
Houston, TX

Three cheeses make this recipe one you'll use again and again.

1 lb. ground beef
14-1/2 oz. can diced tomatoes
10-oz. can diced tomatoes with
    green chiles
6-oz. can tomato paste
2 t. sugar
2 t. salt

1/4 t. pepper
6-oz. pkg. egg noodles, cooked
1 c. sour cream
1 c. shredded Cheddar cheese
1 c. grated Parmesan cheese
1 c. shredded mozzarella cheese

Brown ground beef in a skillet; drain. Stir in tomatoes, tomatoes with chiles, tomato paste, sugar, salt and pepper. Cook 5 minutes over medium heat; lower heat and simmer 30 minutes. Combine egg noodles and sour cream; spread in a lightly greased 13"x9" baking dish. Top with beef mixture; sprinkle with cheeses. Cover with aluminum foil and bake at 350 degrees for 30 minutes. Uncover and bake an additional 5 minutes. Serves 2 to 4.

Dangle sparkling, chunky necklaces around hurricane shades for memorable centerpieces.

Pork Chop Dinner

Laurie Murphy
La Plata, MD

A really good one-pot meal.

6 pork chops
1 T. oil
2 onions, thinly sliced
3/4 c. long-cooking rice,
    uncooked

32-oz. can whole tomatoes
1/2 c. water
1/4 t. sugar
salt and pepper to taste

Brown pork chops lightly in oil in a 2-quart Dutch oven. Top with sliced onions and rice. Add tomatoes with juice, water, sugar, salt and pepper. Bake, covered, at 350 degrees for 1-1/2 hours. Makes 6 servings.

Decorate plain paper cups with ribbons, bows, stickers and flowers...anything but plain!

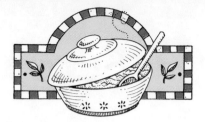

Chicken & Broccoli Alfredo

Joanne Starbuck
Houston, TX

Add some rolls for a complete meal in less than an hour!

4-1/2 oz. pkg. alfredo noodle
   mix
10-3/4 oz. can cream of
   mushroom soup
10-oz. pkg. frozen broccoli
   flowerets, partially thawed

3 to 4 c. cooked chicken, cubed
2 c. shredded Cheddar cheese
6-oz. jar sliced mushrooms,
   drained
6-oz. can French fried onions,
   crumbled

Prepare alfredo noodle mix per package directions. Combine all ingredients except onions in a large bowl; mix well. Spread into a lightly greased 13"x9" casserole dish; top with onions. Bake, uncovered, at 350 degrees for 35 to 40 minutes or until golden and bubbly. Serves 10 to 12.

*Find an old-fashioned chalkboard to announce
"Today's Special." It adds a whimsical diner
feel hanging in the kitchen and lets the whole
family know what's for dinner.*

Cheddar Barbecue

Cheri Emery
Quincy, IL

A hearty meal the whole family will enjoy.

1-1/2 lb. ground beef
1 c. onion, chopped
16-oz. can barbecue-style beans
10-3/4 oz. can tomato soup
1 t. chili powder

1/2 t. salt
1/2 t. paprika
1/4 t. garlic salt
12-oz. tube refrigerated biscuits
1 c. shredded Cheddar cheese

Brown ground beef and onion together; drain. Add beans, soup and seasonings; bring to a boil. Spread mixture into a greased 2-quart casserole dish. Arrange biscuits on top of mixture; sprinkle with cheese. Bake at 375 degrees for 25 to 30 minutes. Serves 6.

Box lunches are a great way to serve up special dinners. Shoe boxes are charming when covered with wallpaper scraps and topped with ribbons and bows.

Baked Chicken Washington

Linda McCaulley
Pittsburgh, PA

Try substituting slices of Muenster cheese for the grated Swiss...it melts beautifully and gives a completely different taste to the same recipe.

1-1/2 c. uncooked rice
1/4 c. all-purpose flour
1 T. chicken bouillon granules
1/4 c. butter, melted
2 c. milk
3 c. cooked chicken, cubed

4-oz. jar sliced mushrooms, drained
1/4 c. green pepper, chopped
2 T. pimento
1 c. shredded Swiss cheese

Prepare rice according to package instructions; set aside. Blend flour and bouillon into butter in a saucepan. Add milk; cook until thickened. Remove from heat and fold in chicken, mushrooms, peppers and pimento. Spread rice in a buttered 8"x8" casserole dish. Top with chicken mixture; sprinkle with cheese. Bake at 350 degrees for 30 minutes. Makes 3 to 4 servings.

Toting goodies to a neighborhood get-together? Try pulling them in a child's wagon or, in winter, on a sled!

Horseradish Pot Roast

Andrea Purdon
Redding, CA

A tasty pot roast recipe with the added kick of horseradish!

4-lb. boneless beef chuck roast
salt and pepper to taste
2 T. oil
1/2 c. onion, chopped

2 c. tomato juice
1/4 c. prepared horseradish
2 T. sherry or water

Sprinkle roast with salt and pepper; brown in hot oil in a Dutch oven.
Remove from Dutch oven and set aside; drain all but one tablespoon
of drippings. Sauté onion in remaining drippings; add tomato juice,
horseradish and sherry or water. Mix well; return meat to pan. Cover;
simmer for 2 to 3 hours or until tender, basting occasionally. Slice
meat and serve with sauce. Serves 12 to 16.

Keep it simple...wrap plastic dinnerware in paper
napkins tied up with colorful ribbons.

Delicious Tuna Quiche

Linda Patten
Lake Zurich, IL

Serve wedges with fresh fruit or a bowl of steaming soup for a dinner everyone will be talking about.

9-inch deep-dish pie crust
6-oz. can tuna, drained
1/2 c. onion, finely chopped
1-1/2 c. shredded Swiss cheese
2 eggs, beaten

1 c. evaporated milk
1 T. lemon juice
3/4 t. garlic salt
1/8 t. pepper
1/4 t. salt

Pierce sides and bottom of pie crust with fork. Bake crust on a baking sheet at 450 degrees for 5 minutes. Spread tuna in pie crust; sprinkle onion and cheese over tuna. Blend eggs, milk, lemon juice and seasonings in a bowl. Pour over tuna-cheese mixture. Place pie on baking sheet; bake at 450 degrees for 15 minutes. Reduce heat to 350 degrees; bake an additional 12 to 15 minutes or until golden. Serves 4 to 6.

Colorful straws layered with slices of kiwi, banana and pineapple are fun fruit skewers for glasses of ice water or frosty lemonade!

can't-Miss Casseroles

Bacon, Turkey & Corn Bake

Karen Lee Puchnick
Butler, PA

If you'd like, substitute ham for the bacon and peas for the corn.

1/2 to 1 lb. bacon, diced
1/2 lb. cooked turkey, finely
   diced
1/2 c. onion, finely diced
1/2 red pepper, roasted and
   diced
1/2 orange pepper, roasted and
   diced
1 c. corn
2 T. fresh parsley, chopped

2 eggs, separated and divided
1-1/4 c. all-purpose flour
1/2 t. baking soda
1 c. buttermilk, divided
1 t. Dijon mustard
1 T. brown sugar, packed
salt and pepper to taste
fresh chives to taste, chopped
1/3 c. shredded Cheddar cheese

Cook bacon, turkey and onion in a skillet over medium heat, stirring often until bacon is slightly crisp and onions are tender. Drain and set aside. Blend peppers, corn and parsley with the bacon mixture; stir gently. Beat egg whites until soft peaks form; set aside. Combine flour, baking soda and 1/2 cup buttermilk in a mixing bowl; stir until smooth. Add egg yolks, remaining buttermilk, mustard and sugar; beat until smooth and light, about 2 minutes. Add salt, pepper and chives to taste. Add egg whites to batter one-half at a time. Spread bacon mixture into the bottom of a 13"x9" baking dish; top with egg mixture. Bake at 350 degrees for 25 minutes; sprinkle with cheese. Continue baking an additional 10 minutes or until golden. Cut into wedges and serve immediately. Makes 8 to 10 servings.

Beef Pot Pie

Tami Transue
Allentown, PA

This tried & true recipe is a great way to use leftover beef or chicken...a tasty homecooked meal for us busy moms!

2 12-inch pie crusts
2 c. stew beef, cooked and cubed
2 10-3/4 oz. cans cream of
    potato soup
1/2 c. milk

1 c. mixed vegetables
salt and pepper to taste
dried parsley, dried thyme and
    onion powder to taste

Line a 12" pie plate with one pie crust. Combine meat, soup, milk and vegetables; season to taste with salt, pepper and seasonings. Spread in pie crust. Top with remaining pie crust; crimp edges and vent top. Bake at 350 degrees for 45 minutes to one hour. Let stand 10 to 15 minutes before serving. Makes 8 servings.

Toss a few refrigerated pie crusts in the cart the next time you're grocery shopping...they're such time savers in either savory or sweet pie recipes!

can't-Miss Casseroles

Taco Pizza

Rachel Fields
Bedford, IN

The kids' favorite...truly a can't-miss dinner idea!

8-oz. pkg. corn muffin mix
1-1/4 oz. pkg. taco seasoning
   mix, divided
1 lb. ground beef, browned
1/2 c. taco sauce

1 c. shredded Cheddar cheese
Garnish: sour cream, chopped
   tomatoes, chopped green
   onion, hot peppers, salsa,
   shredded lettuce

Prepare corn muffin mix according to directions on package; spread in a greased 8"x8" baking dish. Bake at 400 degrees for 6 to 8 minutes. Blend 1/2 package of taco seasoning mix into beef, reserving remaining mix for another recipe. Add any additional ingredients according to taco seasoning mix directions; reducing each by half. Remove cornbread from oven and spread with taco sauce. Top with beef mixture and cheese. Return to oven; continue baking 15 minutes longer or until cheese is melted. Let stand 2 to 3 minutes; cut into squares. Garnish as desired. Serves 2 to 4.

Set up a topping bar when making Taco Pizza...everyone can just help themselves by adding their favorite toppings to individual servings.

Sausage & Bowtie Casserole

Debi DeVore
Strasburg, OH

There's nothing more I can say...it's very, very good!

2 1-lb. rings smoked sausage, sliced and heated through
2 12-oz. pkgs. sliced mushrooms
16-oz. box bowtie pasta, prepared

2 heads cabbage, chopped
1 onion, chopped
1 T. olive oil
salt, pepper and onion powder to taste

Mix all ingredients together in a 3-quart roasting pan. Bake at 375 degrees for 45 minutes until cabbage is tender. Serves 8.

Spruce up dining room chairs in a jiffy by tying a pretty ribbon around the chair back...a snap!

Zesty Roasted Chicken & Potatoes

Denise Mainville
Mesa, AZ

Dinner in a dash!

6 boneless, skinless chicken
   breasts
1 lb. redskin potatoes, quartered
1/3 c. mayonnaise
3 T. Dijon mustard

1/2 t. pepper
2 cloves garlic, pressed
Optional: fresh chives to taste,
   chopped

Arrange chicken and potatoes in a lightly greased jelly-roll pan. Blend remaining ingredients except chives; brush over chicken and potatoes. Bake, uncovered, at 350 degrees for 30 to 35 minutes or until potatoes are tender and juices of chicken run clear. Sprinkle with chives, if desired, before serving. Makes 6 servings.

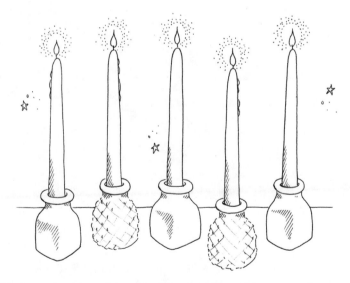

For a pretty glow, take a new spin on vintage inkwells...tuck a taper inside and march them down the center of a buffet table.

Shrimp de Jonghe

Jan Swartzel
Canal Fulton, OH

An elegant seafood dish that's short on prep time.

1/2 c. margarine, melted
2 cloves garlic, minced
1/3 c. fresh parsley, chopped
1/2 t. paprika
1/8 t. cayenne pepper

1/2 c. white wine or chicken
  broth
2 c. soft bread crumbs
2 lbs. cooked shrimp, cleaned

Mix together all ingredients except shrimp in a bowl. Arrange shrimp in a 2-quart casserole dish; top with mixture. Bake at 350 degrees for 25 minutes or until golden. Serves 6 to 8.

Casserole dishes are ideal for sharing with a new mom or new neighbor. For an extra-nice surprise, tuck a few favorite recipes inside an oven mitt and give along with the casserole.

Chicken & Biscuits

Jenn Huber
Valparaiso, IN

Two old-fashioned favorites come together.

2 boneless, skinless chicken
   breasts, cut into bite-size
   pieces
2 T. oil
15-oz. can mixed vegetables,
   drained
10-3/4 oz. can cream of celery
   soup

3/4 c. water
1/2 t. chicken bouillon granules
1 T. Worcestershire sauce
salt to taste
1/4 t. seasoned salt flavor
   enhancer
8-oz. tube refrigerated biscuits

Sauté chicken in oil until no longer pink and juices run clear; drain and set aside. In a microwave-safe dish, combine chicken, vegetables, soup, water, bouillon, Worcestershire sauce and salts; cover. Heat on high for 3 minutes; stir and cook for an additional 2 minutes. Spread into a greased 9"x5" loaf pan. Place biscuits on top; bake at 325 degrees for 20 to 25 minutes or until biscuits are golden. Makes 4 servings.

Tie a colorful bandanna around a warm casserole dish and slip a wooden spoon inside the knot. A clever way to wrap it all up!

Melt-in-Your-Mouth Chicken

Karen Norman
Jacksonville, FL

The buttermilk is the secret ingredient...it keeps the chicken moist.

2 c. cooked chicken, cubed
10-3/4 oz. can cream of chicken
   soup
2 c. chicken broth
1 c. self-rising flour

1 c. buttermilk
1/2 c. butter, melted
1 t. salt
1/2 t. pepper

Arrange chicken in a greased 13"x9" baking dish. Combine soup and broth; mix well and pour over chicken. Mix flour, buttermilk, butter, salt and pepper into a batter; spoon over chicken. Bake for 25 to 30 minutes at 425 degrees. Makes 2 to 4 servings.

Let everyone at the next potluck know what's inside your casserole dish. Glue a beribboned fresh herb sprig to a mailing tag, write the recipe name on the tag and tie onto the casserole lid knob.

Pork Chop-Potato Bake

Janet Allen
Hauser, ID

The French fried onions give this casserole a crispy crunch.

6 pork chops
salt and pepper to taste
2 T. oil
10-3/4 oz. can cream of celery
    soup
1/2 c. milk
1/2 c. sour cream

1/4 t. pepper
24-oz. pkg. frozen hashbrowns
    with onions and peppers,
    thawed
1 c. shredded Cheddar cheese
2.8-oz. can French fried onions

Sprinkle pork chops with salt and pepper; brown in oil and set aside. Combine soup, milk, sour cream, pepper, potatoes and cheese; spread into a 13"x9" baking dish. Top with onions and pork chops; bake at 350 degrees for 45 minutes until bubbly and golden. Serves 6.

Make a stack of simple fabric napkins sparkle...secure each with an old-fashioned clip earring.

Shepherd's Pie

Kimberly Pfleiderer
Galion, OH

Add a can of drained mixed vegetables if you'd like.

2 lbs. ground beef
1/2 onion, chopped
.75-oz. pkg. brown gravy mix
2 10-3/4 oz. cans cream of
   mushroom soup
2-1/2 c. water

salt and pepper to taste
2-1/2 to 3 c. potatoes, peeled,
   boiled and mashed
8-oz. pkg. shredded Cheddar
   cheese

Brown ground beef and onion in a skillet; drain and pour into a mixing bowl. Stir in gravy, mushroom soup and water; mix well. Spread in a 13"x9" baking dish. Sprinkle with salt and pepper. Spread potatoes over top; bake at 350 degrees for 45 minutes. Sprinkle with cheese; bake for an additional 10 minutes or until cheese is melted. Makes 4 to 6 servings.

Spiff up kitchen shelves with homemade paper borders. Cut colorful paper with decorative-edged scissors and attach to shelf edges with double-sided tape...done in no time!

Chicken Pot Pie

Cyndee Masi
Bellflower, CA

Nothing says "home" like the aroma of Chicken Pot Pie.

1/3 c. onion, chopped
1/3 c. butter
1/3 c. all-purpose flour
1/2 t. salt
1/4 t. pepper

1 t. chicken bouillon granules
1-1/3 c. chicken broth
2/3 c. milk
2 c. cooked chicken, diced
2 c. sliced mushrooms

Sauté onion in butter in a saucepan until translucent. Add flour, salt, pepper and bouillon; heat and stir until smooth. Remove from heat; add broth and milk. Bring to a boil; stir in chicken and mushrooms. Set aside. Line a 2-quart baking dish with one pie crust; spoon in chicken mixture. Top with second crust; cut slits in crust. Bake at 425 degrees for 30 to 35 minutes or until golden. Serves 6 to 8.

Pie Crust:

4 c. all-purpose flour
1 T. sugar
2 t. salt
1-3/4 c. oil

1/2 c. water
1 T. white vinegar
1 egg

Blend flour, sugar and salt in large bowl; add oil and mix until crumbly. In a small bowl, beat water, vinegar and egg; pour into flour mixture and mix until moist. Divide into 4 balls; wrap in plastic wrap. Freeze 2 balls for another recipe; chill remaining 2 balls for 30 minutes or more. Roll into crusts.

Country Meatloaf

Jamie Austin
Goose Creek, SC

While I was growing up, my mother made this recipe for our family.
Now I make it for mine and they love it!

1-1/2 lbs. ground beef
1 c. herb-flavored stuffing mix
10-3/4 oz. can cream of
   mushroom soup, divided

1 egg, beaten
1/2 onion, chopped
2 T. sour cream

Combine ground beef, stuffing mix, half the soup, egg and onion; spread in a 9"x5" loaf pan. Bake at 400 degrees for 35 minutes. Mix remaining soup with sour cream; spread over meatloaf. Bake for an additional 5 to 10 minutes. Serves 3 to 4.

Everyone knows mashed potatoes are the perfect side dish for savory meatloaf. Try a delicious secret the next time you make the potatoes...substitute equal parts chicken broth and cream for the milk in any favorite recipe.

Best-Ever Spaghetti Casserole

Dianna Likens
Gooseberry Patch

This just couldn't be any easier!

1 lb. ground sausage
1 onion, diced
14-1/2 oz. can diced tomatoes
10-3/4 oz. can condensed
    tomato soup

2 c. tomato juice
1-lb. pkg. spaghetti, prepared
1 c. shredded Cheddar cheese

Brown sausage and onion together; drain and place in a 13"x9" baking dish. Combine tomatoes, soup, juice and prepared spaghetti; pour over sausage mixture. Top with cheese. Bake, uncovered, at 350 degrees for 45 minutes until cheese is golden and bubbly. Serves 8.

Find a jumbo-size pasta dish for serving up
pasta-filled casseroles...makes helping yourself
so much easier.

Scalloped Sausage & Potatoes

Wanda Garner
Mechanicsburg, PA

A tasty recipe given to me by a friend...now I'm passing it along to you.

4 c. potatoes, peeled, sliced and
    divided
1/4 c. all-purpose flour, divided
1/4 t. salt, divided
1 lb. ground sausage, browned
    and divided

1 c. shredded sharp Cheddar
    cheese, divided
1-1/2 c. milk

Place half the potatoes in a 2-quart casserole dish; sprinkle with half the flour. Top with half the salt, half the sausage and half the cheese; repeat with remaining potatoes, flour, salt, sausage and cheese. Pour milk over the top; cover. Bake at 350 degrees for 50 minutes to one hour; uncover. Bake for an additional 8 to 10 minutes or until potatoes are tender. Serves 4.

Looking for a spectacular centerpiece? Coat a bouquet of roses with spray adhesive, immediately following with a sprinkling of ultrafine iridescent glitter. Gently tap off excess...so sparkly!

can't-Miss Casseroles

Chicken-Artichoke Bake

Kristine Kundrick
Fenton, MI

An impressive dinner in no time. Try it!

2 to 3 lbs. boneless, skinless
    chicken breasts
14-1/2 oz. can chicken broth
14-oz. can artichoke hearts,
    drained and quartered
1/4 c. sliced mushrooms
2 T. butter

1/4 t. salt
1/4 t. pepper
3/4 c. half-and-half
1/2 c. grated Parmesan cheese
1/2 t. dried rosemary
1/4 c. all-purpose flour

Simmer chicken in broth until juices run clear. Place chicken in a 13"x9" baking dish. Top with artichokes and mushrooms; set aside. Combine butter, salt, pepper, half-and-half, cheese and rosemary in a saucepan; bring to a boil. Blend in flour; pour over chicken. Bake at 350 degrees for 30 minutes. Serves 6 to 8.

For something new, try slipping votives inside drinking glasses filled with rock salt and lining them up right across the mantel.

Chicken Enchilada Casserole

May Huffman
Gresham, OR

When I want to try a new version of this favorite recipe, I just dip softened tortillas into the chicken mixture, then layer in a casserole dish. Top with the remaining chicken mixture, then cheese.

16-oz. container sour cream
2 10-3/4 oz. cans cream of
    chicken soup
1/4 c. onion, diced
7-oz. can diced green chiles

2 c. cooked chicken, shredded
salt and pepper to taste
18 6-inch corn tortillas
2 c. shredded Colby cheese
oil for frying

Mix sour cream, soup, onion, chiles, chicken, salt and pepper in a saucepan; simmer until mixture comes to a boil. Remove from heat; set aside. Fry tortillas in oil, one at a time, just until soft; fill each with chicken mixture and roll up. Arrange in a 13"x9" baking dish; sprinkle with cheese. Bake at 350 degrees for 35 to 40 minutes. Serves 6 to 8.

Give your family dinner some fun with a theme...like
serving Chicken Enchilada Casserole
at a Fiesta!

Wild Rice & Turkey Casserole

Leigh Drzycimski
Mason City, IA

*Just right for the day after Thanksgiving, but so good,
you'll want to have it more often!*

2 c. cooked turkey, cubed
6-oz. pkg. long grain and wild
   rice, prepared
10-3/4 oz. can cream of
   mushroom soup

1/2 c. sour cream
1/2 c. onion, chopped
1/3 c. sherry or chicken broth
2 T. butter, melted

Mix all ingredients together; spread in a 13"x9" baking dish. Bake at
350 degrees for 45 minutes. Serves 4.

For the juiciest turkey, slip a quartered orange or
apple inside while roasting.

Easy Beef & Noodles

Linda Pence
Williamstown, KY

*This is the recipe I know I can count on when time is at a premium.
I add a salad, vegetable and dinner rolls to round out the meal.*

10-3/4 oz. can cream of
   mushroom soup
10-3/4 oz. can French onion
   soup

1-lb. stew beef, cubed
8-oz. pkg. egg noodles, prepared

Mix soups together in a 13"x9" casserole dish; add stew beef. Cover
and bake at 350 degrees for 2 hours. Serve over prepared noodles.
Serves 4.

*Looking for something to keep the kids busy while
you're making dinner? Just toss out a roll of kraft
paper and plenty of crayons...they can create a
tablecloth masterpiece!*

can't-Miss Casseroles

Louisiana Shrimp

Deborah DeVaughn
Martin, TN

Ready in 15 minutes!

2 T. butter
1/2 c. Worcestershire sauce
5 cloves garlic, chopped
6 bay leaves, broken in half
2 t. Old Bay seasoning

hot pepper sauce to taste
pepper to taste
2 T. lemon juice
1 lb. shrimp, peeled and cleaned

Combine all ingredients except shrimp in a saucepan; mix well. Bring to a boil; reduce heat and simmer for 5 minutes. Place shrimp in a 13"x9" casserole dish; pour mixture over shrimp. Bake at 400 degrees for 10 minutes. Remove and discard bay leaves. Serves 2 to 4.

Polka dot wrap in a snap! Coat bubble wrap with acrylic paints, then press it onto colored paper...what fun!

Beefy Mexicali Casserole

Amanda Blesi
Vista, CA

Add a side of Spanish rice or refried beans and dinner's ready.

1 lb. ground beef
1 onion, chopped
8-oz. can tomato sauce
10-1/2 oz. can chili
4-oz. can mushrooms, drained
  and chopped

12 6-inch corn tortillas
2-1/4 oz. can sliced black olives,
  drained
2 c. shredded Cheddar cheese
10-oz. can beef broth

Brown beef and onion; drain. Add tomato sauce, chili and mushrooms; set aside. Line a greased 13"x9" baking pan with 6 tortillas; spread half of ground beef mixture, half of the olives and half of the cheese over tortillas. Repeat process, ending with cheese. Pour beef broth over top; cover. Bake at 350 degrees for 30 minutes. Serves 6 to 8.

Give worn quilts a new look as nifty pieced pot holders. Cut 2 squares the same size, pin right sides together and stitch 3 sides. Turn, then stuff with cotton batting and stitch the remaining side closed. Don't forget to add a loop for hanging.

savory
Slow-Cooking

Slow cooking tips & tricks!

* As a time saver, roasts and ground beef don't have to be browned before adding to the slow cooker...they'll be just as tasty.

* For fast cleanup, spray the inside of the slow cooker with non-stick vegetable spray before adding ingredients.

* A leaf of lettuce dropped into the top of a slow cooker will absorb any extra oil from beefy soups and stews...just discard before serving.

* Cut down on prep time by using prepackaged ingredients...scalloped potato mixes, canned tomatoes and soups, seasoning mixes, and frozen vegetables that have been thawed all work well.

* If you're using your slow cooker at high altitudes, be sure to allow an additional 30 minutes for each hour of cooking time specified in the recipe.

* It's easy to put your slow cooker meal together the night before. Just peel and chop up meats and vegetables, then refrigerate in separate plastic zipping bags. The next morning toss everything into the slow cooker.

Easy Veggie Soup

Pamela Berry
Huntington, IN

This is by far my favorite soup. I combined ingredients used by my grandmother, mother and mother-in-law to create this fast and delicious soup recipe!

1 lb. ground beef
1/4 c. dried, minced onion
salt and pepper to taste
12-oz. can cocktail vegetable
   juice
15-oz. can crushed tomatoes

14-oz. can beef broth
2 14-oz. cans mixed vegetables,
   drained
2 T. steak sauce
2 c. water
1 to 2 T. sugar

Brown ground beef with onion; drain. Add salt and pepper to taste; place in a slow cooker. Add vegetable juice, tomatoes, broth, vegetables, steak sauce and water; stir well. Add sugar to taste. Heat on low setting for 6 to 8 hours. Serves 4 to 6.

With work, school, and after-school activities, dinner can be a challenge. Now's the time to get out that slow cooker. Other than a quick chop of a few ingredients, recipes are usually a simple matter of tossing everything into the pot.

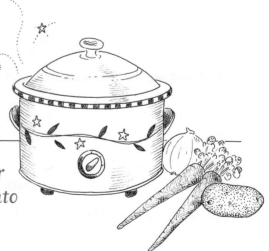

Italian Spaghetti

Jennifer Eveland-Kupp
Temple, PA

This is a "fix it and forget it" dinner for those on the go.

1 lb. ground beef
1 onion, chopped
2 t. salt
1 t. garlic powder
2 15-oz. cans tomato sauce

2-1/2 t. Italian seasoning
1/2 lb. mushrooms, chopped
6 c. tomato juice
8-oz. pkg. spaghetti, uncooked

Brown ground beef with onion; drain. Place all ingredients except spaghetti in slow cooker. Heat 6 to 8 hours on low setting or 3 to 5 hours on high setting. During the last 30 minutes of cooking time, add uncooked spaghetti; cook on high setting until spaghetti is tender. Serves 4.

Instead of adding dry pasta to the slow cooker, boil it until it's just tender, then add.

Creamy Beef Stroganoff

Dawn Allison
Mishawaka, IN

A classic recipe that's oh-so simple.

1 lb. stew beef, cubed
2 10-3/4 oz. cans cream of
   mushroom soup

1-1/2 oz. pkg. onion soup mix
4-oz. pkg. cream cheese
8-oz. pkg. egg noodles, prepared

Combine beef, soup and soup mix in slow cooker; heat on low setting for 8 hours. Stir in cream cheese just before serving; serve over noodles. Makes 4 servings.

Before placing in a slow cooker, sprinkle pork chops or beef with this simple seasoning. Combine one cup salt, 1/4 cup pepper and 1/4 cup garlic powder. Mix all together and store in an airtight container for up to 6 months.

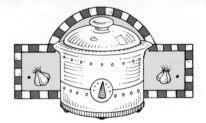

BBQ Ribs

Maureen Gragnani
Garden Grove, CA

I often make this recipe with stew beef and serve over rice or spoon onto buns for sandwiches.

1 onion, sliced
3 to 4 lbs. pork or beef ribs

18-oz. bottle barbecue sauce

Spray inside of slow cooker with non-stick vegetable spray. Add onion slices; top with ribs. Pour sauce over all. Heat on low setting for 8 hours or high setting for 5 hours. Serves 6 to 8.

Remember that slow cookers are sensitive to dramatic changes in temperature. Don't set a hot crock on a cold surface, or fill it with cold water to soak after just removing the hot food inside.

Savory Slow-Cooking

Harvest Beans

Amanda Saner
St. Charles, MO

*A tasty combination of ingredients makes these beans
anything but ordinary!*

16-oz. can kidney beans,
  drained
15-1/2 oz. can butter beans,
  drained
15-oz. can pork & beans
1/2 c. catsup
1 t. mustard

1/2 c. brown sugar or molasses
1/2 c. sugar
1 onion, chopped
1/2 lb. ground beef, browned
1/2 lb. bacon, crisply cooked and
  crumbled

Combine all ingredients, blending well. Place in a slow cooker and heat
on high setting for one hour or until heated through. Serves 4 to 6.

*Slow cookers are ideal for toting to family
reunions...they cook away while everyone spends time
catching up!*

Potato & Corn Chowder

Melody Shane
Whitehall, PA

A hearty, filling chowder that will warm you head-to-toe.

16-oz. bag frozen hashbrowns
15-oz. can corn
15-oz. can creamed corn
1/2 c. onion, chopped
12-oz. can evaporated milk

1-lb. smoked sausage ring,
  sliced
1/2 t. Worcestershire sauce
salt and pepper to taste

Mix all ingredients together; place in a slow cooker. Heat on low setting for 8 hours. Serves 4 to 6.

The mini slow cookers are terrific for making sauces and melting chocolate...keep one on hand.

Shredded Beef Sandwiches

Regina Kostyu
Gooseberry Patch

So good to have for company because you can spend time with them and not in the kitchen. It's also nice to come home to after being at a track meet or soccer game and have dinner ready.

2 to 4-lb. boneless beef chuck
    roast
10-3/4 oz. can cream of
    mushroom soup

1-1/2 oz. pkg. onion soup mix
16 buns

Place roast in slow cooker; spread mushroom soup over top and sprinkle with onion soup mix. Heat on high setting for 4 to 6 hours. Shred and stir with a fork. Spoon onto buns. Serves 12 to 16.

Don't remove the slow cooker lid unless you're checking for doneness or stirring. Every time the cover comes off, you lose heat that is equal to 30 minutes of cooking time, so trust the recipe!

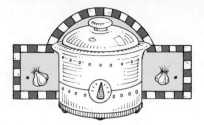

Grammy's Cabbage Rolls

Lisa Ludwig
Fort Wayne, IN

This recipe makes an excellent sauce served over mashed potatoes.

1 head cabbage
1 lb. ground beef, browned
1-1/4 t. salt

1 egg, beaten
1/3 c. instant rice, uncooked

Place cabbage in a saucepan; cover with water and simmer 5 minutes. Drain; carefully remove outer leaves. Combine remaining ingredients, mixing well. Place 1/4 cup mixture on each cabbage leaf and roll up leaf, tucking ends toward center; secure with toothpicks. Place rolls in slow cooker; pour sauce over top. Heat on low setting for 6 to 8 hours or on high setting for 3 to 4 hours. Serves 4.

Sauce:

1 c. onion, thinly sliced
2 t. butter
10-3/4 oz. can tomato soup
1-1/4 c. water
1/2 c. celery, chopped

1 t. fresh parsley, chopped
3 T. lemon juice
1 t. sugar
1 t. salt

Sauté onion in butter until tender. Combine in a saucepan with remaining ingredients; simmer for 10 minutes.

Zesty Macaroni & Cheese

Jen Licon-Conner
Gooseberry Patch

If you want to make this recipe extra zesty, add 1/2 cup salsa
or stir in green chiles to taste!

16-oz. pkg. elbow macaroni,
  prepared
16-oz. pkg. pasteurized
  processed cheese, cubed
8-oz. pkg. Pepper Jack cheese,
  cubed

2 10-3/4 oz. cans Cheddar
  cheese soup
1 c. onion, minced

Pour macaroni, processed cheese and Pepper Jack cheese into slow
cooker. Stir in soup until everything is coated; add onion. Heat,
covered, on low setting for 5 to 6 hours or on high setting for 2 hours.
Stir occasionally. Makes 6 to 8 servings.

A slow cooker makes a super gift! Before wrapping it
up, be sure to tuck in some favorite tried & true
recipes...they'll be so appreciated.

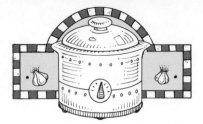

Pizza Casserole

Gloria Shupp
Saylorsburg, PA

Kids big and little will love this cheesy casserole.

1-1/2 lbs. ground beef
1 onion, chopped
12-oz. pkg. rigatoni pasta,
   prepared

28-oz. can pizza sauce
2 lbs. shredded mozzarella
   cheese
20 slices pepperoni, quartered

Brown beef and onion in a skillet; drain. Layer ingredients in order given in a slow cooker. Cover and heat on low setting for 4 to 6 hours. Serves 4.

Slow cookers come in so many sizes, you might want to have more than one! A 3-quart size is handy for sauces and recipes that will feed about four people, while a 5-1/2 quart one is terrific for family reunion-size recipes.

Steak & Rice Casserole

Pat Habiger
Spearville, KS

A hearty casserole recipe you can count on.

2 green peppers, finely chopped
2 celery stalks, finely chopped
4 carrots, peeled and sliced
2 lbs. beef round steak, cut in
　strips
1/2 c. milk

10-3/4 oz. can cream of celery
　soup
10-3/4 oz. can cream of onion
　soup
1-1/2 c. prepared rice

Arrange peppers, celery, carrots and steak in a slow cooker. Mix milk and soups; pour over top. Heat on low setting for 6 hours; add rice and heat on high setting for one hour. Add water or milk if liquid is absorbed. Makes 6 to 8 servings.

Remember to put veggies in the slow cooker first...they actually take longer to cook than the meat or poultry.

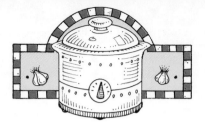

French Dip Au Jus

Terri Vanden Bosch
Rock Valley, IA

Melt-in-your-mouth tender and such flavor!

3 to 4-lb. beef tip roast
2 c. beef broth
2/3 c. brown sugar, packed
1/4 t. seasoning salt

1 t. liquid smoke
1/3 c. soy sauce
6 to 8 hoagie buns
6 to 8 slices Swiss cheese

The day before serving, place roast in a slow cooker and heat on low setting 10 to 12 hours. Let cool; slice thinly across the grain. Arrange slices in a 13"x9" glass baking dish; cover with beef juices from slow cooker. Combine broth, brown sugar, seasoning salt, liquid smoke and soy sauce; heat to boiling. Pour over sliced beef; cover and refrigerate overnight. To serve, return sliced beef and beef juices to slow cooker, set on low and heat through. Serve on hoagie buns with a slice of Swiss cheese and some beef juices for dipping. Serves 6 to 8.

Have a home office? Then tossing tonight's dinner into a slow cooker is a guaranteed way to have a family-style dinner with minimum fuss and preparation throughout the day.

savory Slow-Cooking

Buried Treasure

Angela Frantz
Gig Harbor, WA

Funny name, incredible taste!

2 c. carrots, peeled and sliced
2 c. potatoes, peeled and sliced
1 c. celery, chopped
8-oz. pkg. sliced mushrooms

salt and pepper to taste
1-1/2 lbs. ground beef
14-oz. can chopped tomatoes
1 onion, sliced

Layer carrots, potatoes, celery and mushrooms in a slow cooker; sprinkle with salt and pepper. Place beef over top of vegetables; top with tomatoes and onion. Heat on high setting for 6 to 8 hours. Serves 8.

Why not host a crockery cooking progressive dinner with neighbors? There's only one rule: everyone's dish must be made in a slow cooker!

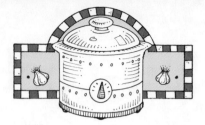

Creamy Chicken Casserole

Jennifer Vander Meersch
Rock Island, IL

This recipe cooks into such a creamy casserole...sure to become a family favorite!

1 pkg. onion flavored frozen
    potato puffs
4 to 6 boneless, skinless chicken
    breasts

10-3/4 oz. can cream of
    mushroom soup

Place potato puffs in slow cooker. Place chicken breasts on top and pour soup over all. Heat on low setting 8 to 10 hours or on high setting 4 to 6 hours. Makes 4 to 6 servings.

Saving time in the kitchen means more time for fun table settings. Sprinkle sequins or rhinestones on the tabletop or fill a glass jar with beads and baubles, then slip a pillar candle inside.

Garlicky Chicken-Mushroom Stew

Amy Butcher
Columbus, GA

Serve with prepared rice and a crispy salad...a winning combination.

4 boneless, skinless chicken
   breasts, cubed
salt and pepper to taste
10-3/4 oz. can cream of
   mushroom & roasted
   garlic soup

3/4 c. water
8-oz. pkg. whole mushrooms
1 c. baby carrots
2 stalks celery, chopped

Arrange chicken in a slow cooker; add salt and pepper to taste. Mix
together soup and water; pour over chicken. Add mushrooms, carrots
and celery; stir gently. Cover and heat on low setting 6 to 8 hours or
until chicken juices run clear when pierced. Serves 4.

Give a busy mom dinner in a dash! Share a
favorite slow-cooking recipe along with all the fixin's
to prepare it. Then, when time's at a premium, she can
toss the ingredients together and forget
about cooking.

Slowly Deviled Beef

Stephanie Mayer
Portsmouth, VA

This cooks all day, but is worth the wait!

2 lbs. stew beef, cubed
1.4-oz. pkg. Sloppy Joe
   seasoning mix
1 c. celery, sliced

1 green pepper, chopped
1/2 c. water
2 T. vinegar
prepared rice or egg noodles

Place all ingredients in slow cooker; stir to mix. Cover and heat about 10 hours on low setting or 4-1/2 to 5 hours on high setting. Serve over prepared rice or noodles. Makes 4 servings.

Dried herbs and spices tend to lose their flavor during long cooking, so it's best to add them at the end of cooking time. Taste and adjust seasonings just before serving.

savory Slow-Cooking

Beef Burgundy

Malacha Payton
Edmond, OK

This elegant dinner is a snap prepared in the slow cooker.

2 lbs. stew beef, cubed
8-oz. can mushrooms, drained
10-3/4 oz. can cream of
   mushroom soup

1-1/2 oz. pkg. onion soup mix
3/4 c. red wine or beef broth
16-oz. pkg. egg noodles,
   prepared

Combine all ingredients in a slow cooker; cover and heat on low setting for 8 to 10 hours. Serve over prepared egg noodles. Makes 4 to 6 servings.

Remember that milk, cheese and sour cream will separate with long cooking, so add them in the last hour of cooking time.

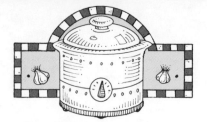

Dad's Tangy Steak Supper

James Lynch
Redfield, IA

I put all these ingredients in the slow cooker before we leave for our soccer tournament. When we get home, there's a wonderful, warm meal waiting for us.

2 lbs. beef round steak, cut into
    serving-size pieces
1/2 c. all-purpose flour
8-oz. bottle French salad
    dressing, divided
salt and pepper to taste

1 onion, chopped
1 green pepper, chopped
Optional: 8-oz. can pineapple
    chunks, drained
3 to 4 c. prepared rice

Roll steak in flour; brown in a skillet with 1/2 cup dressing. Add salt and pepper to taste; arrange in slow cooker. Add remaining dressing, onion, green pepper and pineapple if desired. Cover and heat on low setting for 8 to 10 hours or on high setting for 4 to 6 hours. Serve over prepared rice. Makes 6 servings.

Because the flavor of fresh herbs becomes stronger during slow cooking, try using just half the amount you would normally toss into a similar oven or stove-top recipe.

Slow-Cooking

Barbecue Chicken Wings

Sharon Crider
Lebanon, MO

My family loves it when I make these wings for dinner along with potato salad and baked beans.

3 lbs. chicken wings
1-1/2 c. barbecue sauce
1/4 c. honey

2 t. mustard
1-1/2 t. Worcestershire sauce

Arrange chicken wings on broiler pan. Broil 4 to 5 inches from heat, turning once, about 10 minutes until chicken is golden. Place chicken in slow cooker. Combine barbecue sauce, honey, mustard and Worcestershire sauce in a bowl; mix well and pour over chicken. Cover and heat on low setting for 2 to 2-1/2 hours. Makes about 2-1/2 dozen.

What a great theme for a new cooking club...slow cooking recipes only!

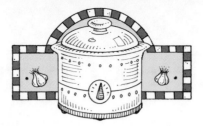

Savory Pork Ribs

Tiffany Brinkley
Broomfield, CO

The sauce is what really makes these ribs stand out from other recipes. Terrific!

1/4 c. soy sauce
1/4 c. orange marmalade
1 T. catsup

1 clove garlic, pressed
3 to 4 lbs. pork ribs, cut into
serving-size pieces

Combine soy sauce, marmalade, catsup and garlic; mix well. Brush over ribs. Arrange in slow cooker; pour remaining sauce over ribs. Cover and heat on low setting for 10 to 12 hours. Serves 6 to 8.

Box up Savory Pork Ribs in take-out containers and deliver to a friend...what a welcome surprise.

savory Slow-Cooking

Swiss Steak Supper

Darcy Geiger
Columbia City, IN

Swiss Steak Supper is one of those classics you just can't go wrong with. Substitute mashed potatoes for cooked egg noodles if you'd like.

3 lbs. boneless beef round steak,
   cut into serving-size pieces
seasoning salt to taste
2 onions, sliced
1 green pepper, sliced

1 c. baby carrots
14-1/2 oz. can brown gravy
46-oz. can tomato juice
16-oz. pkg. egg noodles, cooked

Sprinkle beef with seasoning salt; brown in skillet sprayed with non-stick vegetable spray. Layer beef, onions, green pepper and carrots in slow cooker. Combine gravy and tomato juice in a bowl; mix well and pour over beef and vegetables. Cover and heat on low setting for 10 to 12 hours. Serve over prepared noodles. Makes 6 servings.

Don't forget slow cookers make great traveling companions for campers. Enjoy all the fun of the great outdoors, then come in for a delicious dinner.

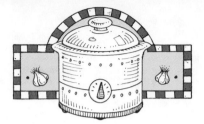

Tangy Italian Sausage

Ronda Miller
Elizabethtown, PA

Split hoagie buns and fill with sausages and sauce for a really tasty fair-style dinner.

2 to 3 lbs. Italian sausage links
1 c. onion, sliced
1 c. green pepper, sliced
1 c. water

48-oz. jar spaghetti sauce
6-oz. can tomato paste
1 T. grated Parmesan cheese
1 T. fresh parsley, minced

Cover sausages with water in a 10-inch skillet. Bring to a boil; reduce heat and simmer for 10 minutes. Drain. Stir remaining ingredients together in a slow cooker; add sausage. Heat on low setting for 3 to 4 hours. Serves 4 to 6.

Use a permanent black marker for printing names onto the smoothest rocks you can find...clever placecards for a family picnic.

Sticky Chicken

Deborah Byrne
Clinton, CT

I think this is the best chicken recipe...you have to try it!

4 t. salt
2 t. paprika
1 t. cayenne pepper
1 t. onion powder
1 t. dried thyme

1 t. white pepper
1/2 t. garlic powder
1/2 t. pepper
3 to 4-lb. chicken, skin removed
1 c. onion, chopped

Mix the first 8 ingredients together; rub chicken all over with mixture. Place chicken in a resealable plastic zipping bag and refrigerate overnight. The next morning, sprinkle onion in the bottom of a slow cooker; place chicken on top. Heat on low setting for 8 hours. Serves 4.

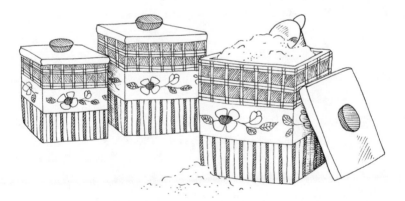

It's simple to whip up a sauce to thicken slow cooker dishes. Whisk 2 to 4 tablespoons of flour or cornstarch into 1/4 cup cold water until smooth and stir into a simmering slow cooker.

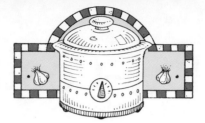

Chicken Supreme

Jeanne Calkins
Midland, MI

Mom would make this dish all the time while I was growing up.
Now, when I make it for my family, the aroma takes
me back to my childhood.

2-1/2 oz. pkg. dried, chipped
   beef
8 boneless, skinless chicken
   breasts
8 slices bacon

1/2 c. sour cream
1/4 c. all-purpose flour
10-3/4 oz. can cream of
   mushroom soup
12-oz. pkg. pasta, cooked

Arrange dried beef to cover the bottom and lower sides of a slow cooker. Wrap each piece of chicken with a slice of bacon and arrange on top of dried beef; some pieces of chicken may overlap. In a small bowl, thoroughly blend sour cream, flour and soup. Pour mixture over chicken. Cover and heat on low setting for 8 to 10 hours or on high for 5 hours. Serve over hot buttered pasta of choice. Serves 8.

Don't heat up the oven for yummy baked potatoes...make them in the slow cooker! Pierce 6 to 12 potatoes with a fork and wrap each in aluminum foil. Add to the slow cooker, cover and cook on low setting 8 to 10 hours or on high setting 2-1/2 to 4 hours.

Mexicali Rice

Marian Buckley
Fontana, CA

Serve this with chicken or turkey breasts to make it even heartier!

15-1/4 oz. can corn, drained
15-oz. can black beans, drained
   and rinsed
4-oz. can diced green chiles
1 onion, chopped
1 red pepper, chopped
2 c. long-cooking rice, uncooked
3-1/2 c. boiling water

1/2 c. frozen orange juice
   concentrate
4-1/2 T. lime juice, divided
1-1/2 T. ground cumin
1 T. chili powder
1/3 c. fresh cilantro, chopped
1/2 t. salt

Combine corn, black beans, chiles, onion, pepper, rice, water, orange juice, 1/4 cup lime juice, cumin and chili powder in a slow cooker. Cover and heat on low setting for 2-1/2 to 3 hours. Stir in remaining lime juice, cilantro and salt; mix well. Serves 4 to 6.

Make a family recipe book of all the best handed-down family favorites. Tie it all up with a bow and slip a family photo in the front...a gift to be treasured.

Easy Roast Beef Sandwiches

Cynthia Holtz
Park Forest, IL

This recipe takes 10 hours to cook, so turn it on first thing in the morning and forget about it until dinnertime.

4 to 5-lb. beef chuck roast
.7-oz. pkg. Italian salad dressing
8 to 10 pepperoncinis

2 c. hot water
16 to 20 buns

Combine all ingredients except buns in a slow cooker; heat on low setting for 10 hours. Shred beef; serve on buns. Serves 16 to 20.

Add a little something special to the dinner table tonight. Try rolling a linen napkin, securing with pretty ribbon and then slipping a sweet blossom under the ribbon.

Broccoli-Cheese Soup

Kathy Smith
Cincinnati, OH

My daughters would eat this every day if I made it!

2 10-oz. pkgs. frozen broccoli
   cuts, thawed
2 10-3/4 oz. cans cream of
   celery soup

2 c. half-and-half
8-oz. jar pasteurized processed
   cheese sauce
2 cubes chicken bouillon

Mix all ingredients in a slow cooker. Heat on low setting for 5 to
6 hours. Makes 4 to 6 servings.

Stack two pie plates or a pair of bowls, inverting the
bottom one, to vary the height of goodies being
served on the table...makes it easier to see what might
be "hiding!"

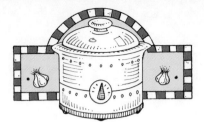

Potato Soup

Sheila Cottrell
Loveland, OH

I love to make this for my family on snowy winter days.

8 to 10 potatoes, peeled and
   diced
1 carrot, peeled and diced
1 onion, diced
3 to 5 c. water

4 cubes chicken bouillon
1 t. dried parsley
1/2 t. garlic, minced
1/3 c. margarine
12-oz. can evaporated milk

Place potatoes, carrot and onion in slow cooker with water, bouillon cubes, parsley, garlic and margarine; cover. Heat on low setting for 10 to 12 hours or on high setting for 4 to 5 hours. During the last hour of cooking, stir in the evaporated milk. Makes 6 to 8 servings.

Mix & match colors of Fiesta® tableware for a real splash of color guests will love.

Hearty Beef Stew

Connie Knepp
Yeagertown, PA

Filled with vegetables, this recipe is a good way to
get the kids to eat their veggies!

3 carrots, peeled and sliced
3 potatoes, diced
1 onion, chopped
2 stalks celery, sliced
2 lbs. stew beef, cubed
1/4 c. all-purpose flour
1-1/2 t. salt
1/2 t. pepper

1 clove garlic, minced
1 bay leaf
1 c. beef broth
1 t. Worcestershire sauce
1 t. paprika
2 t. browning and seasoning
   sauce

Arrange vegetables in a slow cooker; top with beef and set aside. Mix flour, salt and pepper; sprinkle over meat. Stir well; add remaining ingredients. Cover; heat on low setting for 8 to 10 hours or on high setting for 4 to 5 hours. Remove and discard bay leaf. Serves 4 to 6.

It's easy to convert your favorite stew recipe from stove top to slow cooker. If it usually simmers 35 to 45 minutes, that equals 6 to 8 hours on low or 3 to 4 hours on high. Recipes that cook one to 3 hours will be done in 8 to 16 hours on low or 4 to 6 on high.

Anything Goes Chili

Wendy Leonard
Travis AFB, CA

Add A-B-C-shaped pasta for the little ones.

1 lb. ground beef, browned
14-1/2 oz. can diced tomatoes
   with garlic and onion
14-1/2 oz. can stewed tomatoes
15-1/2 oz. can kidney beans,
   drained

15-1/4 oz. can corn, drained
garlic to taste
29-oz. can tomato sauce
2 to 3 c. prepared pasta

Combine all ingredients in a slow cooker; heat on low setting for 4 hours. Stir in prepared pasta 30 minutes before serving. Serves 4 to 6.

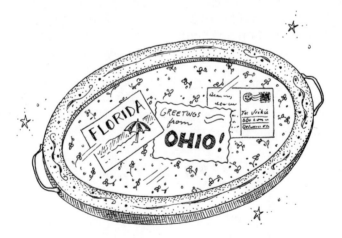

A large oval picture frame with flat glass makes a smart serving tray. Slip family photos or postcards under the glass, then set on bowls of everyone's favorite chili toppers so they can help themselves!

Meatless Mains

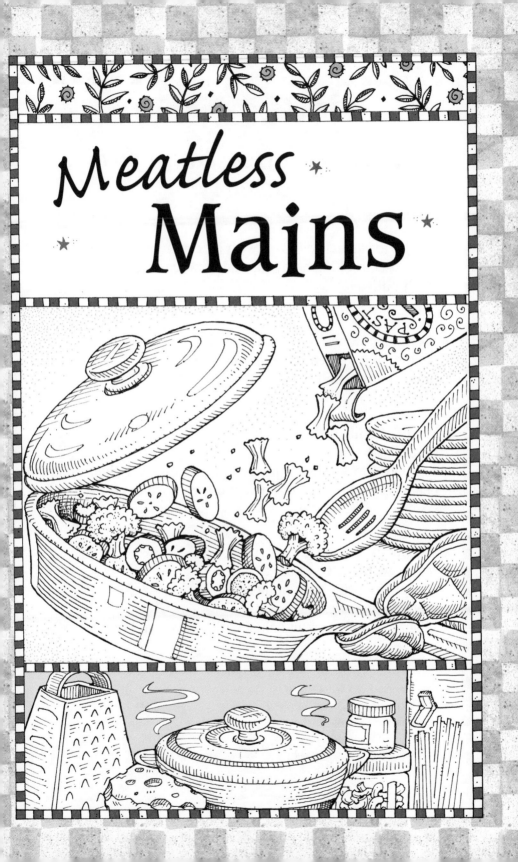

Cutting calories, saving time... so easy!

⋆ Grill a toasted cheese sandwich by coating the skillet with non-stick cooking spray instead of spreading the bread with butter.

⋆ Save time...don't soak and cook dried beans, buy canned varieties you can quickly drain and rinse.

⋆ Make a terrific meatless sauce for pasta in no time...sauté 6 chopped tomatoes, 3 chopped green onions, 1 chopped green pepper, 15-oz. can of drained and rinsed white beans, 1/2 cup

⋆ Instead of buying garlic bread made with butter, create a warm-from-the-oven homemade version to serve with pasta dishes. Simply spread baked garlic cloves on French bread.

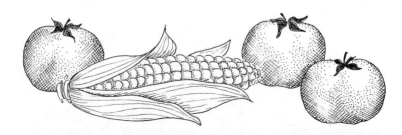

★ *Meatless* Mains

Zucchini Casserole

Lynn Bauter
Lake Oswego, OR

I make this recipe all the time…it's a huge hit at parties, family get-togethers or when we have friends visit.

10 zucchini, thinly sliced
2 c. shredded mozzarella cheese
7-oz. can diced green chiles
2 c. shredded Cheddar cheese

3/4 c. biscuit baking mix
1/2 c. milk
1 egg, beaten
grated Parmesan cheese to taste

Lightly oil a 13"x9" baking dish and layer as follows: one-third of the zucchini slices, mozzarella cheese, chiles, one-third zucchini slices, Cheddar cheese, remaining zucchini. Combine biscuit baking mix, milk and egg; spread over top of casserole. Sprinkle with Parmesan and bake at 350 degrees for one hour, until golden. Serves 6 to 8.

Keep centerpieces whimsical. A pillar nestled in a sand-filled bowl and surrounded by seashells has a terrific summertime look.

Garden Pie

Kathy Grashoff
Fort Wayne, IN

A veggie dish filled with all the best harvest from the garden.

4 c. yellow squash, sliced
8-oz. pkg. sliced mushrooms
1 green pepper, sliced
1 red pepper, sliced
1 onion, sliced
1 clove garlic, minced
1/4 c. olive oil
1 t. salt

1/2 t. white pepper
1/8 t. cayenne pepper
4 eggs
1/2 c. half-and-half
4-oz. pkg. Gruyere cheese,
    shredded
3/4 c. grated Parmesan cheese
9-inch pie crust

In a large skillet, sauté squash, mushrooms, peppers, onion and garlic in oil over medium-high heat for 10 minutes. Transfer vegetables with a slotted spoon to a bowl. Sprinkle vegetables with salt and pepper; stir until well blended. Beat together eggs and half-and-half; stir in cheeses. Pour 2/3 cup of egg mixture into crust. Spoon in half of the vegetables. Continue layering, ending with egg mixture. Bake at 375 degrees for 35 to 40 minutes or until top is golden and filling is set. Cool on rack for 30 minutes; serve warm. Makes about 8 servings.

Keep the garden theme by serving wedges of Garden Pie in new wax paper-lined terra-cotta saucers.

⋆ *Meatless* Mains

Eggplant Roma

Roberta Miller
Washington, DC

A scrumptious way to enjoy eggplant...try adding a couple of plants to your summertime garden so it's always on hand.

2 T. olive oil
3 cloves garlic, minced
1/3 c. onion, chopped
2 to 2-1/2 c. eggplant, peeled
   and cubed

1 c. grape tomatoes, halved
salt and pepper to taste
2 to 3 T. balsamic vinegar
1 T. dried basil

Heat oil and garlic over medium heat; add onion. Cook for 5 to 6 minutes or until tender; stir in eggplant, tomatoes, salt and pepper. Reduce heat; cook for 10 minutes or until eggplant is tender; pour in vinegar and basil. Cook for an additional 5 minutes. Serves 2.

Give that new, plain lampshade a one-of-a-kind look...just pick up some stencils and paint at a local home improvement store and decorate the shade to match your home.

Black Bean & Pepper Enchiladas

Nicole Biddison
Scotts Valley, CA

A great alternative to meat-filled enchiladas, and they're so tasty!

1 T. oil
1 T. garlic, minced
2 peppers, sliced
1 onion, sliced
15-oz. can black beans, drained
   and rinsed

16-oz. can enchilada sauce,
   divided
10 6-inch flour or corn tortillas
4 c. shredded sharp Cheddar
   cheese

Add oil to a skillet and sauté garlic, peppers and onion. Cook until onion is transparent. Remove from heat and place in a bowl; add black beans. Pour half the enchilada sauce into a 13"x9" baking dish. Fill tortillas with 2 to 3 tablespoonfuls of the bean and vegetable mixture; sprinkle with cheese. Roll tortillas and place seam-side down into baking dish. Top with remaining enchilada sauce and any remaining cheese. Bake at 350 degrees for 30 minutes. Serves 4 to 6.

Looking to save a few calories? It's so easy when serving Mexican-style foods. Reduced-calorie sour cream and cheeses are perfect garnishes that taste great.

⋆ Meatless Mains ⋆

Stir-Fry Vegetables

Jen Licon-Conner
Gooseberry Patch

You just can't go wrong with this stir-fry recipe...it's a snap!

3/4 c. pineapple juice
1 T. sugar
1 T. lemon juice
1-1/2 t. cornstarch
1 t. soy sauce
4 t. oil
1 c. broccoli flowerets

1 c. carrot, peeled and sliced
1 c. cauliflower flowerets
1 c. celery, sliced
1 c. red pepper, cut into bite-size
  pieces
1 c. sugar peas, stemmed

Combine first 5 ingredients in a bowl; mix well and set aside. Heat oil in a skillet; add broccoli, carrots, cauliflower and celery and cook for 2 minutes over medium-high heat. Add pepper and sugar peas; heat an additional 2 minutes. Add pineapple juice mixture. Cover and bring to a boil; continue boiling for one minute. Serves 4 to 6.

Handy gadgets like mini choppers make prep work a breeze for chopping potatoes, onions, eggs, tomatoes or peppers...what a time saver!

Herbed Zucchini & Pasta

Cathy Karnes
Manhattan Beach, CA

A fix-it-fast dish your family will love.

2 T. butter
1/4 c. plus 2 T. oil, divided
1 clove garlic, minced
1 onion, chopped
1 green pepper, diced
3 zucchini, halved lengthwise
    and sliced

1 t. dried parsley
1 t. dried rosemary
1 t. dried basil
16-oz. pkg. bowtie or ziti pasta,
    prepared
1/2 c. grated Parmesan cheese

Melt butter with 2 tablespoons oil in a skillet; add garlic and onion. Sauté for 5 minutes; stir in green pepper and sauté for an additional 3 minutes. Stir in zucchini and herbs; heat for 5 to 8 minutes or until zucchini is tender. Add remaining oil; toss with pasta. Sprinkle with Parmesan cheese. Serves 4.

Use craft glue to adhere colorful buttons around the bottom of a pillar candle...a quick-as-a-wink gift Grandma is sure to love.

✱ Meatless Mains

Mock Crab Cakes

Karen Lee Puchnick
Butler, PA

Yes, they do taste like crab cakes! A recipe that came in handy while trying to decide what to do with the overabundance of zucchini in Dad's garden.

2 c. zucchini, coarsely grated
2 T. onion, grated
2 T. celery, finely chopped
2 T. green pepper, finely chopped
1 T. mayonnaise
1 T. Worcestershire sauce
1 T. Old Bay seasoning
2 eggs, beaten
2 c. soft bread crumbs
2 T. butter
Garnish: lemon wedges, tartar
　　sauce

Press zucchini in a length of cheesecloth to remove as much moisture as possible. Combine with next 7 ingredients. Lightly fold in bread crumbs; gently form into patties that are 3 inches in diameter and one inch thick. Melt butter in a skillet; fry patties over medium heat until golden on both sides. Serve with lemon wedges and tartar sauce, if desired. Makes 8 to 10 servings.

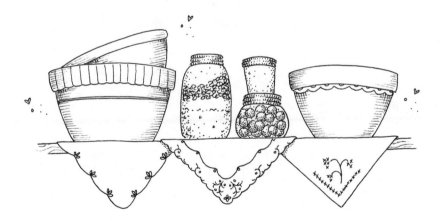

Old-fashioned handkerchiefs make sweet shelf edging. Drape them over a shelf, letting the pretty stitching hang down over the edge.

Vegetable Ribolitta

*Lynda McCormick
Burkburnett, TX*

*This soup is traditionally thickened with bread such
as toasted croutons or crostini.*

1 c. sweet onion, chopped
2/3 c. celery, chopped
2/3 c. baby carrots, sliced
3 to 4 cloves garlic, minced
2 T. olive oil
2 19-oz. cans cannellini beans,
   drained
32-oz. can vegetable broth
4 c. cabbage, chopped

2 14-1/2 oz. cans diced Italian
   tomatoes
1/4 c. red pepper, diced
1/4 c. yellow pepper, diced
1/2 c. zucchini, diced
1 t. fresh thyme, chopped
Garnish: grated Parmesan
   cheese

Sauté onion, celery, carrots and garlic in olive oil until tender. Add
beans, broth, cabbage, tomatoes, peppers, zucchini and thyme.
Simmer over medium heat for about 20 minutes or until vegetables are
tender. To serve, place a slice of crostini in each bowl and ladle soup
into bowl. Sprinkle with Parmesan cheese. Serves 8.

Crostini:

1/2 c. olive oil
1/8 t. salt
1 t. Italian seasoning

1 loaf Italian bread, cut into
   one-inch slices

Combine first 3 ingredients; brush onto one side of each slice of bread.
Arrange bread on a baking sheet, coated side up. Bake at 375 degrees
for 15 minutes until lightly toasted.

*Share the garden bounty! A market basket of fresh
veggies makes a terrific gift for a friend or neighbor.*

✴ *Meatless* Mains

Roasted Asparagus with Feta

Denise Neal
Yorba Linda, CA

Sometimes I add freshly chopped basil, garlic and bow tie pasta...delicious any way you make it!

1 bunch asparagus, trimmed
1 to 2 t. olive oil
coarse salt to taste

2 tomatoes, chopped
8-oz. pkg. crumbled feta cheese

Arrange asparagus spears in a 2-quart baking dish; sprinkle with olive oil and add salt to taste. Bake at 400 degrees for 15 to 20 minutes or until tender; let cool. Chop into 2-inch pieces and toss with tomatoes and feta cheese. Serves 4.

To keep a bouquet of pretty blossoms fresh, add a spoonful of sugar and a little lemon-lime soda to the water.

79

Gnocchi with Mushroom Sauce

Kristy Rangel
Racine, WI

Gnocchi are little Italian dumplings made from potatoes and other ingredients. They're used much like pasta, either in soups or with sauces...give them a try!

2 cloves garlic, minced	1/2 t. salt
1 T. oil	1/2 t. pepper
3 c. sliced mushrooms	12-oz. pkg. gnocchi, prepared
1 c. vegetable broth	2 T. grated Parmesan cheese
1 t. dried rosemary	

Sauté garlic in oil in a skillet for 2 minutes. Add mushrooms; cook until tender. Stir in broth, rosemary, salt and pepper; reduce heat and simmer until liquid is almost absorbed. Spoon over prepared gnocchi. Sprinkle with Parmesan cheese. Serves 4.

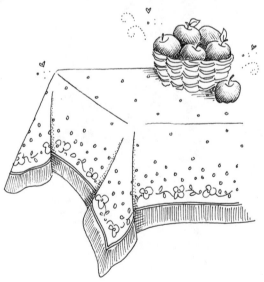

Centerpieces don't need to be fussy...fresh fruit tucked into a basket, bowl or vintage colander always looks (and tastes) terrific!

Meatless Mains

Ravioli Lasagna

Karen Lee Puchnick
Lyndora, PA

Almost everyone loves lasagna, but not the work involved. A friend shared this recipe with me and it's fabulous! Prep time is also short enough to make it a tasty weeknight meal.

2 c. pasta sauce, divided
16-oz. container ricotta cheese
10-oz. pkg. frozen chopped
   spinach, thawed and drained
2 eggs, beaten
salt and pepper to taste

1/2 c. grated Romano or
   Parmesan cheese
18-oz. bag frozen cheese ravioli
1/2 c. shredded mozzarella
   cheese

Spread 1/2 cup pasta sauce in a 5" deep, 8"x8" baking dish. In a bowl, blend ricotta, spinach, eggs, salt, pepper and Romano or Parmesan cheese. Layer one-third of the ravioli in the baking dish; top with half the ricotta mixture. Repeat layering, ending with remaining third of ravioli. Spoon remaining pasta sauce over top; sprinkle with mozzarella. Cover with aluminum foil and bake at 375 degrees for 40 minutes. Remove foil and continue baking an additional 10 minutes. Makes 4 servings.

Life is a combination of magic and pasta.

-Federico Fellini

Zinbeanie Bow Ties

Elizabeth Thompson
Aberdeen, NJ

If you like the taste of anchovies, you can add a teaspoon of anchovy paste with the onion and garlic.

1/4 c. olive oil
1 sweet onion, chopped
3 cloves garlic, chopped
1 t. salt
1/2 t. pepper
1/2 t. Italian seasoning
2 T. fresh parsley, chopped
15-oz. can black beans, drained and rinsed
14-1/2 oz. can diced tomatoes
2 T. balsamic vinegar
1/2 c. white wine or vegetable broth
16-oz. pkg. bowtie pasta, prepared
Garnish: 1/2 c. grated Parmesan cheese

Heat olive oil in a large skillet. Add onion and garlic; sauté until tender. Add salt, pepper, Italian seasoning, parsley, beans, tomatoes, vinegar and wine or broth. Reduce heat to low; cover and simmer 20 minutes. Add prepared pasta to skillet; heat and stir for 2 to 3 minutes. Place in a large serving bowl and top with Parmesan cheese. Serves 4 to 6.

For tomatoes to keep their fresh-from-the-garden taste, they should always be stored at room temperature.

Mushroom Crust Quiche

*Karin Geach
Elk Grove, CA*

*A tried & true family favorite from my mother. She made a
brilliant impression upon my childhood...she shone for me like
the evening star and I loved her dearly.*

5 T. butter, divided
8-oz. pkg. mushrooms, chopped
1/2 c. saltine crackers, crushed
1/4 c. green onions, chopped
2 c. shredded Monterey Jack
  cheese

1 c. small-curd cottage cheese
4 eggs
1/4 t. pepper
1/4 t. paprika

Melt 3 tablespoons butter over medium heat in a large skillet. Add
mushrooms and heat for 6 minutes or until soft. Stir in cracker
crumbs; pour into a well-greased 9" pie plate. Press evenly over
bottom and up sides to form crust; set aside. In a small saucepan,
melt remaining butter over medium heat; add onions and heat for
5 minutes or until soft. Spread over crust; sprinkle evenly with cheese.
In a blender, combine cottage cheese, eggs and pepper; blend until
smooth. Pour into crust and sprinkle with paprika. Bake at
350 degrees for 25 to 35 minutes or until a knife inserted just off
the center comes out clean. Let stand 15 minutes before serving.
Makes 6 to 8 servings.

*Set a vintage stained glass window on a sill...so
pretty when the sun shines through!*

Creamy Penne Pasta

Linda Romano
Canonsburg, PA

In no time you have a quick, easy and delicious meal.

2 8-oz. cans tomato sauce
garlic powder to taste
white pepper to taste
1 c. half-and-half

1 T. grated Parmesan cheese
16-oz. pkg. penne pasta, cooked
Garnish: fresh parsley, chopped
    and grated Parmesan cheese

Pour tomato sauce, garlic powder and pepper into a small saucepan.
Stir in half-and-half and cheese. Simmer over low heat until heated
through. Place prepared pasta in a large serving bowl; top with sauce.
Garnish with parsley and cheese. Serves 4 to 6.

*Scented geraniums or pots of herbs placed by the door
give off a delicate aroma that will make guests, and
family, feel so welcome.*

Vegetarian Chili

Julia Spigelmeyer
Elizabethtown, PA

Filling and so yummy!

4 t. olive oil
3 onions, chopped
28-oz. can crushed tomatoes
2 c. vegetable broth
1-1/2 c. cracked wheat
19-oz. can kidney beans, rinsed
    and drained

19-oz. can cannellini beans,
    rinsed and drained
2 c. corn
1 green pepper, chopped
4 t. chili powder
1/2 t. salt
1/4 t. cayenne pepper

Heat oil in a saucepan; add onions and cook until softened. Stir in tomatoes, broth and cracked wheat. Bring to a boil; reduce heat and simmer until cracked wheat is tender. Stir in the remaining ingredients. Bring to a boil; reduce heat and simmer, uncovered, until heated through. Serves 8.

Clever placecards...rubber stamp names on twill tape, tie around a rolled-up napkin and place in the center of each plate.

Risotto with Asparagus

*Suzie Raymond
South Bend, IN*

*Risotto should stand only briefly before being served to keep
this pasta-like rice dish creamy and rich.*

2 14-1/2 oz. cans vegetable
   broth
2 T. olive oil
1 c. onion, chopped
1 c. celery, thinly sliced
2 cloves garlic, minced

1-1/2 c. Arborio rice, uncooked
1 lb. asparagus, trimmed and cut
   into 1-1/2 inch pieces
1/3 c. grated Parmesan cheese
1 T. butter, softened

Measure broth; add enough water to make 5-3/4 cups liquid. Bring to
a simmer in a saucepan; reduce heat to low. Heat oil in a large skillet;
add onion, celery and garlic. Sauté for 4 to 5 minutes, until onion is
translucent; add rice and stir for one minute. Add one cup hot broth;
simmer, stirring often, until liquid is almost completely absorbed, about
4 minutes. Repeat with 2 additional cups hot broth, adding one cup at
a time. Add asparagus and another cup hot broth; cook and stir until
absorbed. Add another cup broth; cook and stir until rice and
asparagus are tender-firm. Remove from heat; stir in cheese, butter
and remaining 3/4 cup hot broth. Let stand briefly before serving.
Serves 3 to 5.

*Check out flea markets for vintage linen sheets. They
can double as tablecloths or, simply draped over a
rod, quick, elegant curtains.*

✳ *Meatless* Mains

Vegetable Paella

Tonya Sheppard
Galveston, TX

Paella is one of the most famous Spanish dishes... give it a try, you'll love it!

1 c. dried cannellini beans
1 c. dried lima beans
2 T. olive oil
1-2/3 c. tomato, chopped
1 c. red pepper, chopped
1 c. yellow pepper, chopped
3/4 c. onion, chopped
3/4 c. zucchini, diced
3/4 c. yellow squash, diced
1 T. fresh rosemary, chopped

2 cloves garlic, minced
3 14-1/2 oz. cans vegetable broth
2/3 c. water
1/3 c. sliced kalamata olives
1/2 t. saffron or turmeric
1 t. paprika
1/2 t. salt
1/4 t. pepper
3 c. prepared wild rice

Sort and rinse beans; place in a large Dutch oven. Cover with water to 2 inches above beans; bring to a boil and cook 2 minutes. Remove from heat; cover and let stand one hour. Drain beans and set aside. Heat oil in a large Dutch oven over medium heat. Add next 8 ingredients; sauté 5 minutes or until tender. Add beans, broth, water and next 5 ingredients; cover. Reduce heat and simmer one hour or until beans are tender. Stir in prepared rice and simmer an additional 3 minutes or until heated through. Serves 6 to 8.

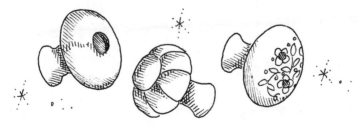

Small glass knobs and drawer pulls make lovely dish-towel hangers in the kitchen...just attach the screws into a peg board.

Creamy Penne with Swiss Chard

Jen Burnham
Delaware, OH

A lightly spiced pasta dish that's ready to serve in 30 minutes.

16-oz. pkg. penne pasta,
  uncooked
1 bunch Swiss chard, trimmed
  and sliced
1 T. butter
2 onions, sliced
3 cloves garlic, minced

1/4 t. red pepper flakes
1/8 t. nutmeg
1 c. ricotta cheese
1/3 c. vegetable broth
1/4 t. salt
1/2 c. oil-packed, sun-dried
  tomatoes, sliced

Cook pasta according to package directions; add Swiss chard 2 minutes before end of cooking time. Drain; set aside. Melt butter in a skillet over medium-high heat; add onions, garlic, pepper flakes and nutmeg. Heat until onion is tender, about 10 minutes. In a blender, purée ricotta with broth and salt until smooth. In serving bowl, combine ricotta mixture with onion mixture, tomatoes and pasta mixture; toss to coat. Makes 6 servings.

Look for vintage photo frames at flea markets and tag sales...their whimsical styles and colors are fun paired with the kids' school pictures or family snapshots.

⋆ Meatless Mains ⋆

Rigatoni with Cannellini & Kale

Jill Valentine
Jackson, TN

An elegant dish that's a snap to prepare.

2-1/2 c. rigatoni, uncooked
2 T. olive oil, divided
3 garlic cloves, minced
7-oz. jar roasted red peppers,
    drained and sliced
1/2 lb. kale, coarsely chopped

16-oz. can cannellini beans,
    drained
2 T. lemon juice
1/4 t. pepper
6 T. grated Parmesan cheese

Cook pasta according to package directions. Drain, reserving
1/4 cup cooking liquid; set aside. Heat one tablespoon oil in a Dutch
oven over medium heat. Add garlic and peppers; sauté one minute.
Add kale and cannellini beans; cover and cook 5 minutes
or until kale is wilted, stirring occasionally. Add prepared pasta,
reserved cooking liquid, remaining oil, lemon juice and pepper; stir
well. Sprinkle with Parmesan cheese. Serves 6.

*What a terrific centerpiece! Fill a bell jar with colorful
veggies...red radishes, orange peppers and green
Brussels sprouts.*

Ratatoûille

Ginny Paccioretti
Oak Ridge, NJ

A southern French dish made with eggplant, zucchini, onions, peppers, tomato and garlic. There are many different varieties, but this recipe is my favorite!

1 onion, chopped
3 to 4 cloves garlic, chopped
3 to 4 T. olive oil
2 zucchini, sliced
2 eggplants, peeled and cubed
2 green peppers, sliced

28-oz. can crushed tomatoes
1 t. dried parsley
1 t. dried oregano
1 t. dried basil
4 c. prepared rice

Sauté onion and garlic in olive oil. Add remaining ingredients; simmer on medium heat for 30 minutes or until vegetables are tender. Serve over prepared rice. Serves 6 to 8.

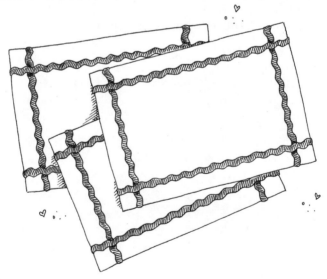

For a quick-to-stitch placemat, transform plain placemats with a trim of rick-rack.

Cheesy Vegetable Pasta

Lisa Mayfield
Branchburg, NJ

This recipe is so delicious! I make it with tricolor rotini or even spinach pasta.

2 to 3 cloves garlic, chopped
2 T. butter
2 yellow squash, sliced
2 zucchini, sliced
1/4 c. white wine or vegetable
   broth

1/2 lb. pasteurized processed
   cheese spread, sliced
2 c. milk
pepper to taste
12-oz. pkg. rotini pasta, cooked

Sauté garlic in butter for 2 minutes. Add squash and zucchini; sauté for an additional 2 minutes. Add wine or broth; lower heat and simmer until tender. In another saucepan, heat cheese spread, milk and pepper until cheese is melted; stir well. Top pasta with vegetables and cheese mixture; toss to coat. Serves 3 to 4.

Cookie cutters are the cutest napkin rings and make fun take-home gifts for guests.

Vegetable Fettuccine

Karen Lehmann
New Braunfels, TX

Add any variety of vegetables you like best.

3 zucchini, cut into strips
3 carrots, peeled and cut into
   strips
1 c. sliced mushrooms
1 clove garlic, minced
1/4 c. butter
1/2 t. dried basil
1/2 t. salt

8-oz. pkg. fettuccine, uncooked
8-oz. pkg. spinach fettuccine,
   uncooked
1 c. grated Parmesan cheese,
   divided
2 egg yolks
1 c. whipping cream

Sauté vegetables and garlic in butter for 5 minutes. Stir in basil and salt; set aside. Prepare fettuccine and half of spinach fettuccine, reserving other half for another recipe; combine with vegetables and spoon into a Dutch oven. Simmer until heated through, stirring occasionally. Add 3/4 cup cheese; blend well. Beat egg yolks and whipping cream together until foamy; add to fettuccine mixture and toss gently. Cook over medium heat until mixture thickens. Sprinkle with remaining cheese before serving. Serves 6 to 8.

Tea towels from the 1940's are perfect bread basket liners and add a splash of color to any table.

Meatless Mains

Cheesy Baked Eggplant

Karen Pilcher
Burleson, TX

*Looking for something new to do with your eggplant?
Try this recipe!*

1-lb. eggplant, peeled and cubed
1 c. dry bread crumbs
1/2 c. evaporated milk
1/4 c. milk
1/4 c. onion, minced
1/4 c. green pepper, minced
1/4 c. celery, minced
1/4 c. butter

2 eggs, beaten
1 T. pimento, chopped
2 t. salt
1/2 t. pepper
1/4 t. dried sage
1-1/2 c. shredded Cheddar
   cheese

Cover cubed eggplant with water; refrigerate for at least 6 hours.
Drain; place in a saucepan. Cover with water; simmer until tender and
set aside. Soak bread crumbs in evaporated milk and milk. In a skillet,
sauté onion, pepper and celery in butter for 15 minutes. Stir in bread
crumb mixture and eggplant. Add eggs, pimento, salt, pepper and
sage; blend well. Spread in a greased 13"x9" baking pan; bake at
350 degrees for 45 minutes. Sprinkle with cheese; heat an additional
5 to 6 minutes until cheese melts. Serves 6 to 8.

*Look for old restaurant serving
dishes at flea markets
and antique
shops...they're roomy
enough to hold the
largest family recipes.*

Baked Spinach Mostaccioli

Kathy Grashoff
Fort Wayne, IN

Easy to make and disappears like magic!

16-oz. pkg. mostaccioli pasta,
   cooked and divided
10-oz. pkg. frozen spinach,
   thawed and drained

8-oz. pkg. mushrooms, halved
2 28-oz. jars spaghetti sauce
2 c. shredded mozzarella cheese

Place half of prepared mostaccioli in a 2-1/2 quart casserole dish; top with spinach and mushrooms. Arrange remaining mostaccioli over mushroom mixture; pour spaghetti sauce over top. Sprinkle with cheese; bake at 350 degrees for 30 minutes. Serves 12 to 16.

To clean fresh spinach easily, place the leaves in a pan of lukewarm water. After a few minutes, drain and discard the water, then repeat if needed.

No-Noodle Lasagna

Carolyn Pindell
Galloway, OH

A time-saving version of an all-time favorite.

16-oz. container ricotta cheese
1/2 c. grated Romano cheese
1 t. dried basil
1 t. dried oregano
1 T. fresh Italian parsley, chopped
1/2 t. pepper
1 lb. zucchini, sliced lengthwise and divided

1 lb. eggplant, peeled, sliced lengthwise and divided
26-oz. jar spaghetti sauce, divided
2 c. shredded mozzarella cheese, divided

Combine ricotta cheese, Romano cheese, basil, oregano, parsley and pepper in a large bowl; stir well. Lightly spray a 13"x9" baking dish with non-stick cooking spray. Layer in order half of the following: zucchini, ricotta cheese mixture, eggplant, pasta sauce and 1/2 cup mozzarella cheese. Repeat layering, ending with 1/2 cup mozzarella cheese. Bake at 375 degrees for 40 minutes. Remove from oven and top with remaining cheese. Bake for an additional 5 to 8 minutes, until cheese is melted and golden. Let stand 15 minutes before serving. Makes 4 to 6 servings.

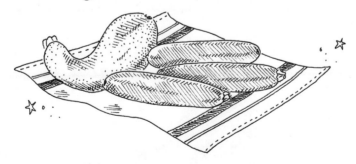

Zucchini and other summer squash make tasty main dishes and are easily swapped out in recipes. Try substituting yellow crookneck or pattypan for zucchini in any favorite recipe.

Easy Veggie Lasagna

Nancy Likens
Wooster, OH

Already chopped frozen veggies keep prep time short.

1/2 c. onion
1 T. oil
28-oz. jar spaghetti sauce
16-oz. pkg. frozen cauliflower,
   carrot and asparagus blend,
   thawed and drained
4-oz. jar sliced mushrooms
16-oz. container cottage cheese

1 egg, slightly beaten
1/2 c. grated Parmesan cheese,
   divided
6 strips lasagna, uncooked
8-oz. pkg. shredded mozzarella
   cheese
1/4 c. water

Heat onion in oil in a skillet over medium-high heat until crisp tender. Add spaghetti sauce, vegetables and mushrooms; stir to combine. Set aside. In a medium bowl, combine cottage cheese, egg and 1/4 cup Parmesan cheese; blend well. Spread one cup spaghetti sauce mixture in an ungreased 13"x9" baking dish. Top with 3 uncooked strips lasagna, half of the cottage cheese mixture, half of remaining spaghetti sauce mixture and half of the mozzarella. Repeat layers, starting with lasagna. Pour water around edges of baking dish and sprinkle with remaining Parmesan cheese; cover tightly with foil. Bake at 375 degrees for 45 minutes or until bubbly. Uncover; bake an additional 10 minutes. Let stand at least 5 to 10 minutes before serving. Serves 6 to 8.

Meatless Mains

Fettuccine Alfredo

Dora Finley
Kennett, MO

There's nothing like creamy fettuccine and this is a winning recipe.

1/2 c. butter
1 c. grated Parmesan cheese
1 pt. whipping cream

fresh parsley to taste, chopped
garlic salt to taste
16-oz. pkg. fettuccine, cooked

Melt butter in a skillet over medium-low heat; add cheese. Mix well; stir in cream until thick. Sprinkle with parsley and garlic salt to taste; pour over prepared fettuccine. Serves 4 to 6.

Try drizzling homemade basil pesto over warm
Fettuccine Alfredo for fresh-from-the-garden taste!
Just blend 2 cups basil, 2 cloves of garlic, 1/2 cup
grated Parmesan cheese and 1/2 cup olive oil in the
food processor...delicious!

Spinach-Swiss Pie

Elaine Slabinski
Monroe Township, NJ

Serve with fresh fruit and dinner's ready in no time.

10-oz. pkg. frozen chopped
   spinach
1 c. shredded Swiss cheese
2 T. onion, chopped
1-1/2 c. milk

3 eggs
3/4 c. biscuit baking mix
1 t. salt
1/4 t. pepper
1/8 t. nutmeg

Cook spinach according to package directions; drain well. Mix spinach, cheese and onion in a bowl; pour into a greased 9" pie plate. Combine milk, eggs, biscuit baking mix, salt, pepper and nutmeg in a blender and blend until smooth. Pour over spinach mixture. Bake at 350 degrees for 45 to 50 minutes or until a knife inserted into center comes out clean. Serves 6 to 8.

Salad's perfect paired with any main dish, so plant lots of leaf lettuce in your garden this year. Just trim off what you need and the plant will continue to grow and give you crispy lettuce all summer long.

✴ *Meatless* Mains

Garden-Veggie Sandwiches

Kathy Fortune
Wooster, OH

For a new taste, replace the mustard with flavored cream cheese.

2 to 4 t. Dijon mustard
2 whole-grain English muffins,
   split and toasted
1/2 c. small broccoli flowerets

1/4 c. red pepper, chopped
1/4 c. carrots, shredded
1/4 c. shredded Monterey Jack
   cheese

Spread mustard over cut side of each muffin half; arrange broccoli, peppers and carrot over mustard. Sprinkle with cheese and place English muffin halves on a broiler pan. Broil about 4 inches from heat for 2 to 3 minutes until cheese melts. Serve immediately. Makes 2 servings.

For a tasty change when making a grilled cheese sandwich, add thin slices of cucumber, tomato, onion, mushrooms and green pepper along with the cheese, then grill as usual...yummy!

Golden Rice Pie

Kim Gillen
Mohnton, PA

Mushrooms and spinach combine perfectly with Swiss cheese.

8-oz. fresh mushrooms, chopped
1 t. garlic, minced
2 T. olive oil
10-oz. pkg. frozen spinach,
    thawed

2 c. prepared rice
1 c. sour cream
1 c. shredded Swiss cheese
salt and pepper to taste

Sauté mushrooms and garlic in olive oil; add spinach. Cook until separated; set aside. In a bowl, combine rice, sour cream, cheese, salt and pepper; spread half of mixture in the bottom of a greased 13"x9" baking dish. Top with mushrooms and spinach; add remaining rice. Bake at 375 degrees for 45 minutes or until golden. Serves 4 to 6.

Don't forget to visit the farmers' market for the best homegrown veggies...toss a market basket in the car and let the kids pick out fresh flavors for dinner tonight!

Very Veggie
Sides & Salads

Make it fresh & fast!

★ You can easily substitute sour cream for mayonnaise in any favorite potato or macaroni salad

★ For a delicious flavor and fewer calories in tuna or chicken salad recipes, combine Dijon mustard with plain yogurt and add salt and pepper along with fresh or dried herbs to taste.

★ Whip up a 3-Bean Salad in no time...drain and rinse one, 15-oz. can each of garbanzo, kidney and green beans. Mix with your favorite low-fat dressing.

★ A make-ahead tossed salad that will be fresh and crisp...ideal for a family get-together! Prepare a salad using any favorite fresh vegetables, except for sliced tomatoes (they'll get too soft). Spoon the salad into a water-tight container, cover the salad with water and secure lid. Refrigerate and drain before serving.

★ If you're cutting up some veggies for dinner, go ahead and cut some extra to tuck into the kids' lunchboxes for tomorrow. Less work in the morning!

very Veggie Sides & Salads

Sweet Potato Casserole

Jackie Crough
Salina, KS

Sweet potatoes with a crunchy golden topping.

40-oz. can sweet potatoes,
    drained
3/4 c. sugar
2 eggs, beaten

1/3 c. evaporated milk
1/4 c. margarine, melted
1 t. vanilla extract

Mash sweet potatoes; blend in remaining ingredients. Spread in 13"x9" baking dish. Spread topping over top; bake at 300 degrees for 35 minutes. Serves 8 to 10.

Topping:

1/3 c. margarine, melted
1 c. brown sugar, packed

1/2 c. all-purpose flour
1 c. nuts, chopped

Blend together margarine, sugar and flour; add chopped nuts and stir.

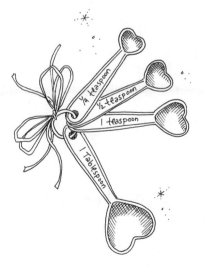

Instead of marshmallows, try topping a favorite sweet potato casserole recipe with canned, sliced peaches and cashews. Sure to be a hit!

Shoepeg & Green Bean Casserole
Kathie McWherter
Bentonville, AR

A new spin on a traditional side dish.

15-oz. can shoepeg corn,
    drained
14-1/2 oz. can green beans,
    drained
10-3/4 oz. can cream of celery
    soup

1 c. sour cream
1 c. shredded Cheddar cheese
1 c. round buttery crackers,
    crushed
1/2 c. butter, melted

Mix corn, beans, soup, sour cream and cheese together; spread in a greased 2-quart casserole dish. Top with cracker crumbs; drizzle butter over top. Bake at 350 degrees for one hour or until golden. Makes 6 to 8 servings.

Why not try a light substitution? Low-fat plain yogurt or cottage cheese is just as tasty as sour cream.

very veggie Sides & Salads *

Cucumber Salad

Patricia Jarman
Valrico, FL

Garden fresh and fast!

1 T. oil
1 t. dried parsley
2 to 3 T. sour cream
2 to 3 T. vinegar
1/2 t. dill weed

1 onion, sliced
2 to 3 cucumbers, peeled and
  sliced
salt and pepper to taste

Mix first 5 ingredients together; blend well. Add onion and cucumbers; salt and pepper to taste. Chill at least one hour. Serves 4 to 6.

Dress up Cucumber Salad with a fancy deviled egg garnish. Use any favorite recipe and instead of slicing the eggs in half lengthwise, set them on their ends. Make a zig-zag cut across the top half and scoop out the insides.

Santa Fe Vegetable Salad

Laurel Perry
Grayson, GA

A veggie salad with a sassy dressing!

1 zucchini, diced
1/2 c. corn, drained
5 green onions, chopped
1 red pepper, chopped

1 jicama, peeled and diced
1/3 c. chunky salsa, drained
1/3 c. fresh cilantro, chopped
salt and pepper to taste

Combine all ingredients together; toss with dressing. Serves 4 to 6.

Dressing:

1/3 c. lime juice
2 T. hot pepper jelly

1 T. water
1 T. oil

Mix all ingredients together in a saucepan; heat until jelly melts.
Stir well.

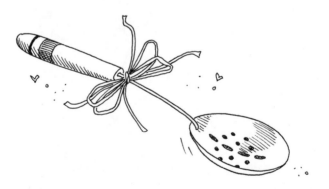

*Fresh veggies don't need to be fussy. A simple raw
vegetable antipasto means forgetting about plates
and forks with a tasty pick-up-and-munch snack.*

Roasted Potatoes with Tomatoes

Yvonne Higgins
Frankin, NH

Layers of tender potatoes and herbs.

6 potatoes
1 t. olive oil
6 plum tomatoes, sliced

1 T. chives, minced
1 T. fresh rosemary, minced
salt and pepper to taste

Bake potatoes in microwave on high setting for 15 to 20 minutes until done, but still firm. Peel and slice crosswise into 1/2-inch thick slices. Arrange potatoes in a well-oiled, shallow 2-quart baking dish. Alternate layers of potatoes and tomatoes; drizzle lightly with olive oil and sprinkle with herbs, salt and pepper. Bake at 375 degrees for 20 to 25 minutes or until potatoes are golden and begin to turn crisp around the edges. Serves 6.

For a low-calorie supper, turn a veggie side dish into a flavorful supper. Make the servings larger than usual and add a crisp salad alongside.

Easy Summer Broccoli Salad

Lori Pearson
Orem, UT

Sprinkle in almonds or raisins too...you just can't miss with this!

2 c. broccoli flowerets
1 c. seedless red grapes
1/4 c. sunflower seeds
1/2 c. sweetened, dried
    cranberries
3/4 c. coleslaw dressing

Mix all ingredients together; toss well. Serves 4.

Dress up dinner with green onion starbursts. Cut the green tops into long, thin slices. Soak in ice water for 15 minutes and they'll curl open.

Swiss Potato Kugel

Keli Morris
Sacramento, CA

*You can always substitute another cheese for Swiss...try
Cheddar or mozzarella.*

1 c. onion, minced
2 T. butter
4 c. potatoes, peeled and diced
2 c. shredded Swiss cheese
1/4 c. all-purpose flour

1 t. salt
1/4 t. pepper
3 eggs
3/4 c. half-and-half

Sauté onion in butter until tender; remove from heat. Stir in potatoes;
set aside. Combine cheese, flour, salt and pepper; add to potato
mixture. Beat eggs and half-and-half together in another bowl; mix
into potatoes. Spread in a greased 9"x9" baking pan; bake, uncovered,
at 350 degrees for 20 to 30 minutes. Let cool 5 minutes before
serving; cut into squares. Makes 4 to 6 servings.

*Stack 2 cake plates for serving a variety of dinner
rolls in style.*

Garden-Fresh Vegetable Bake

Michele Hastings
Bedford, TX

Hearty and filling.

4 yellow squash, chopped
4 zucchini, chopped
2 T. olive oil
1 bunch green onions, chopped
4 to 5 cloves garlic, minced
10-3/4 oz. can cream of chicken
   soup
1/4 c. milk

8-oz. pkg. cream cheese,
   softened
14-3/4 oz. can creamed corn
8-oz. pkg. shredded Cheddar
   cheese
salt and pepper to taste
6-oz. pkg. garlic croutons

Combine squash and zucchini in a saucepan; cover with water and simmer about 5 minutes. Transfer to a skillet. Stir in olive oil, onions and garlic; sauté until tender. Place in a mixing bowl; add soup, milk, cream cheese, corn, cheese, salt and pepper. Mix well; spoon into a 13"x9" baking dish. Bake at 350 degrees for 35 minutes; sprinkle with croutons. Bake for an additional 20 minutes or until golden and bubbly. Serves 6 to 8.

For a whimsical table tent, slip a card under the handle of an old-fashioned cookie cutter.

Parmesan-Basil Vegetables

Pamela Boland
Fort Rucker, AL

Remember to make ahead of time and chill so the flavors can blend.

2/3 c. mayonnaise
1/3 c. grated Parmesan cheese
2 T. vinegar
1 t. dried basil
1 clove garlic, minced
2 c. broccoli flowerets

1-1/2 c. cauliflower flowerets
1 zucchini, cubed
1 carrot, peeled and sliced
1 onion, sliced and separated
    into rings

Mix mayonnaise, cheese, vinegar, basil and garlic together; stir in vegetables. Cover and refrigerate for 2 hours. Serves 3 to 4.

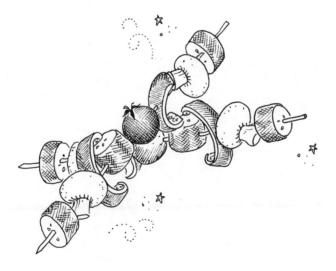

An oh-so simple kabob sauce is equal parts soy sauce, orange juice and olive oil. Add a sprinkle of ginger and sugar if you'd like...quick & tasty!

Spinach Squares

Amy Davila
Fowlerville, MI

I find these cheesy squares make a great side or main dish.

4 c. shredded Cheddar cheese
10-oz. pkg. frozen chopped
    spinach, thawed
1 c. all-purpose flour
2 eggs, beaten

1 c. milk
1 t. salt
1 t. baking powder
1/2 c. onion, chopped
1/4 c. butter, melted

Blend together all ingredients. Spread in a lightly oiled 13"x9" baking dish. Bake at 350 degrees for 35 minutes. Let cool slightly; cut into squares. Makes 9 to 12 servings.

Invite the neighbors over for a casual dinner and let everyone help in the preparations. What a terrific way to swap and try new recipes!

very veggie Sides & Salads

Delicious Cauliflower Casserole

Kim Neideigh
Elizabethtown, PA

A veggie dish even the kids will love!

1/2 c. butter, melted
20-oz. pkg. frozen cauliflower
    flowerets, thawed
1/4 lb. pasteurized processed
    cheese spread, cubed

1/2 c. milk
salt to taste
1/2 sleeve round buttery
    crackers, crushed

Layer butter, cauliflower and cheese in a 2-quart casserole dish. Pour milk over cheese; sprinkle with salt and cracker crumbs. Bake, covered, at 375 degrees for 45 minutes. Serves 4 to 6.

Serve up crispy salads in bread bowls...it's a snap!
Hollow out mini loaves of round bread and they're
ready to fill. The bread pulled from the center can be
torn and crisped under the broiler for tasty croutons.

Sweet Onion & Zucchini Bake

Paula Allen
Menomonee Falls, WI

I tell everyone this is an excellent recipe!

3 c. sweet onion, thinly sliced
3 c. zucchini, thinly sliced
1/4 c. butter
2 eggs, beaten
1/4 c. milk

1 t. salt
1/8 t. pepper
1/4 t. dry mustard
1 c. shredded Swiss cheese,
   divided

Sauté onion and zucchini in butter until tender. Arrange in a shallow 1-1/2 quart baking dish. Combine eggs, milk, salt, pepper, mustard and 1/2 cup cheese. Pour egg mixture over vegetables; sprinkle with remaining cheese. Bake at 375 degrees for 20 minutes or until center is set. Makes 6 servings.

Keeping the menu all veggie? Round off a veggie main with special cheeses and breads along with glasses of sparkling water...relax and enjoy.

Very Veggie Sides & Salads

Grilled Vegetable Salad

Kathy Unruh
Fresno, CA

A versatile salad you can serve warm or cold.

1/4 c. balsamic vinegar
3 cloves garlic, chopped
2 T. fresh basil, chopped
1 T. pepper
3/4 c. olive oil
1 eggplant, peeled and sliced
4 portabella mushrooms
1 sweet onion, sliced
2 zucchini, sliced lengthwise

2 yellow squash, sliced
   lengthwise
1 red pepper, roasted and cut
   into thin strips
4-oz. smoked mozzarella cheese,
   diced
salt to taste
Garnish: fresh basil

Whisk together vinegar, garlic, basil, pepper and oil in a large bowl; toss with vegetables. Marinate at room temperature for at least 30 minutes; drain, reserving 1/2 cup marinade. Grill vegetables over very high heat for 4 to 8 minutes or until crisp-tender; chop coarsely. Place in a bowl; add reserved marinade. Stir in cheese; sprinkle with salt. Serve warm or chilled, garnished with basil. Serves 8.

A veggie grinder is a wonderful spin on the traditional meat-filled sub sandwich. Load layers of veggie slices on kaiser rolls, then top with low-fat or no-fat Italian dressing.

Stuffed Sweet Peppers

Elsie Mellinger
Annville, PA

These crunchy raw stuffed peppers are a family recipe that's kid approved...that says it all!

3 c. bread, torn
1 c. Colby, Muenster or
  American cheese, diced
1/2 c. mayonnaise-style salad
  dressing

2 t. sugar
1/4 t. Worcestershire sauce
4 green peppers, stemmed and
  halved

Combine bread, cheese, salad dressing, sugar and Worcestershire sauce, blending well. Divide mixture equally among pepper halves. Serves 4 to 8.

Turn any simple salad into a pretty layered salad. Just add favorite salad ingredients, one layer at a time, into a glass serving bowl. Toss with dressing just before serving.

Summary Salad

Vickie Streich
Belgrade, MT

There's nothing like fresh tomatoes and cucumbers from the garden!

2 cucumbers, diced
6 tomatoes, diced

1 red onion, diced

Mix all ingredients together; toss with dressing. Serves 6 to 8.

Dressing:

1/2 c. mayonnaise-type salad
    dressing
1/4 c. Catalina salad dressing
1/4 c. whipping cream

1 T. sugar
1 t. salt
pepper to taste

Combine all ingredients; mix well.

A can't-go-wrong mix of vintage and new tableware is always a fun and different way to serve up dinner.

Peanutty Slaw

Judy Forgey
Edmonds, WA

Great for toting to any get-together...always a must-have!

4 c. cabbage, shredded
1 c. cauliflower, chopped
1 c. sour cream
1 c. mayonnaise
1 T. vinegar
1 t. salt
1 T. sugar

1/4 c. green onion, chopped
1/4 c. green pepper, chopped
1/2 c. cucumber, chopped
1 T. margarine, melted
1/2 c. Spanish peanuts
2 T. grated Parmesan cheese

Combine cabbage and cauliflower; set aside. Mix sour cream, mayonnaise, vinegar, salt, sugar, onion, pepper and cucumber together; stir into cabbage mixture. Set aside. Stir margarine, peanuts and cheese together; add to cabbage mixture. Serves 8 to 10.

Keep the week's running menu at a glance. Tack extra-wide rick-rack to a bulletin board and just slip the grocery list underneath.

Surprise Spring Salad

Barbara Vanarsdall
Hilliard, OH

Try cashews or slivered almonds instead of walnuts.

1 red pear, cored, quartered and sliced
1-1/2 T. balsamic vinegar
1 c. mixed greens

3 T. grated Parmesan cheese
2 T. fresh mint, chopped
1 t. chopped walnuts
2 t. olive oil

Marinate pears in vinegar for 5 minutes, tossing to coat; drain, reserving vinegar. Place equal amount of greens on 2 salad plates; top with pears, cheese, mint and nuts. Set aside. Combine reserved vinegar with oil; drizzle over salad. Serves 2.

Drop in a few sweetened, dried cranberries in place of raisins in your next salad...a sweet-tart version that's terrific.

Confetti Corn Chip Salad

Barb Crowe
Lima, OH

Packed with color and flavor!

2 16-oz. cans pinto beans,
    drained and rinsed
1/2 c. onion, chopped
1 tomato, diced
1 c. red pepper, diced

1 c. green pepper, diced
1 c. yellow pepper, diced
16-oz. bottle Catalina dressing
10-oz. pkg. corn chips

Mix all ingredients together; stir well and serve immediately. Serves 8 to 10.

*Serve up fruit salads in old-fashioned glass compotes
so all the colors show through.*

Garden-Fresh Veggie Bundles

Shirley Flanagan
Wooster, OH

An easy foil packet recipe...so simple and no clean-up.

2 c. potatoes, cubed
2 c. zucchini, sliced
1 c. carrots, sliced
1 c. red pepper, diced
1 c. green pepper, diced
1 c. broccoli flowerets, chopped

1 c. sweet onion, diced
1 to 2 ears corn, cut into 6 pieces
1/4 c. vegetable oil
1 T. Cajun seasoning, divided
garlic salt to taste

Spray 6 sheets of heavy duty aluminum foil with cooking spray. In a large bowl, combine first 8 ingredients; toss with oil. Evenly divide vegetable mixture among prepared foil. Sprinkle each vegetable packet with 1/2 teaspoon Cajun seasoning and garlic salt to taste. Bring sides of foil to center and fold over to seal. Fold ends to center, creating a tight bundle. Repeat with all packets. Place bundles on a baking sheet; bake at 450 degrees for 30 minutes or until vegetables are tender. Serves 6.

Serve crisp salads in hollowed-out oranges or avocados or spooned over quartered tomatoes for a tasty change.

Healthy Hummus

Terri Webber
Miami, FL

A popular taste from the Mediterranean.

3 green onions, sliced
4 cloves garlic, chopped
15-1/2 oz. can chickpeas
fresh parsley to taste
2 T. vegetable broth
2 T. lemon juice

1/2 t. pepper
1/8 t. hot pepper sauce
1 t. olive oil
Garnish: carrot sticks, toasted
    pita wedges

Combine all ingredients in a food processor; process until smooth.
Serve with carrot sticks or toasted pita wedges. Serves 2 to 4.

*Try hummus as a healthy spread on sandwiches instead
of mayonnaise. Serve on broiled fish or chicken or even
to top baked potatoes instead of sour cream.*

Very Veggie Sides & Salads

Cottage Salad

Shirley Olson
Harlon, IA

Our daughter, Julie, took this salad to the Iowa State Fair when she was 12 years old and won second place!

1 c. broccoli flowerets
1 c. cauliflower flowerets
1 to 2 T. water
1 carrot, peeled and shredded
1 green onion, diced
1/4 c. radishes, sliced

1/4 c. green pepper, sliced
12-oz. container cottage cheese
1/4 t. dill weed
1/8 t. garlic powder
1/8 t. dry mustard
4 leaves lettuce

Heat broccoli and cauliflower in water over medium heat until crisp-tender. Drain and let cool. Combine remaining ingredients except lettuce in a bowl. Mix lightly and stir in cooled vegetables. Cover and refrigerate until chilled. Spoon onto lettuce leaves. Makes 4 servings.

Red-ripe tomatoes make delicious salad bowls. Cut a slice from the top of the tomato and use a spoon to scoop out the seeds. Cut the tomato edge into scallops or a zig-zag pattern, sprinkle with salt, invert on paper towels and chill. Fill right before serving.

Veggie Lover's Delight

Kathleen Smith
Pflugerville, TX

Filled with good-for-you favorites!

2 cloves garlic, minced
1 serrano pepper, minced
2 c. broccoli flowerets
5 mushrooms, sliced
1 yellow squash, sliced
1 zucchini, sliced

1 green pepper, sliced
1 red onion, sliced
2 T. butter
2 c. spinach, stemmed
1 c. shredded Monterey Jack
  cheese

Sauté garlic, pepper, broccoli, mushrooms, squash, zucchini, green pepper and onion in butter for 7 to 10 minutes or until tender. In skillet, alternate layers of spinach and sautéed vegetables; sprinkle with cheese. Cover; heat for 3 to 5 minutes or until cheese melts. Serves 4.

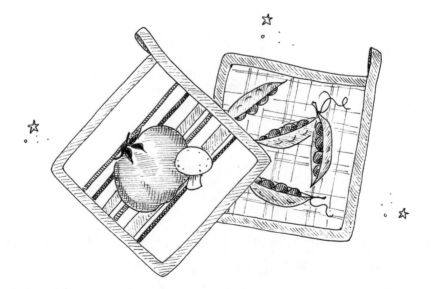

For a no-fuss meal, spoon sautéed veggies onto a softened tortilla and roll up...delicious!

Golden Mushroom Casserole

Karen Pilcher
Burleson, TX

An easy-to-make recipe prepared the night before.

1/4 c. butter
1-1/2 lbs. sliced mushrooms
1 onion, chopped
1/2 c. celery, chopped
1/2 c. green pepper, chopped
1/2 c. mayonnaise
8 slices bread, cubed and
    divided

2 eggs, beaten
1-1/2 c. milk
10-3/4 oz. can cream of
    mushroom soup
1 c. grated Romano cheese

Melt butter in a skillet; add mushrooms, onion, celery and pepper. Heat until tender; drain well. Stir in mayonnaise; set aside. Place half of the bread cubes in a greased 13"x9" baking pan; spoon mushroom mixture over bread cubes. Top with remaining bread; set aside. Combine eggs and milk; pour over all. Cover and refrigerate for 8 hours. Spread soup over top; sprinkle with cheese and bake at 350 degrees for one hour. Serves 6.

Wherever you go, no matter what the weather, always bring your own sunshine.

-Anthony D'Angelo

Savory Orzo Dish

Bev Eckert
Jonesboro, AR

Add more garlic if you really like the flavor.

2 T. butter
2 cloves garlic, minced
1-1/2 c. orzo pasta, uncooked
1-1/2 oz. pkg. savory herb
   soup mix

4 c. water
8-oz. pkg. sliced mushrooms
2 T. fresh parsley, chopped

Melt butter in a skillet; add garlic and pasta. Heat until golden, stirring constantly. Stir in soup mix and water; simmer for 10 minutes. Add mushrooms; simmer for 10 minutes or until liquid is absorbed. Stir in parsley. Makes 2 to 4 servings.

Use packaged mashed potatoes as a tasty time saver for any meal. To give them a special taste, stir in a little cream cheese and sour cream while warming up. Garnish with a sprinkle of paprika before serving.

Very Veggie Sides & Salads

Oriental Fried Rice

Michelle Campen
Peoria, IL

I think this makes the tastiest side dish.

2 T. oil
3-1/2 c. prepared rice, chilled
2 T. soy sauce

1/4 c. green onions, thinly sliced
1 egg, beaten

Heat a non-stick skillet or wok. Add oil and heat over medium heat until just smoking. Carefully add rice, stir in soy sauce and onions. Cook and stir for 5 minutes. Add egg; heat and stir just until egg has cooked through. Makes 4 servings.

Old-fashioned oil & vinegar bottles make great gifts for any salad lover. Tie on a tag with a few favorite salad dressing recipes and wrap them up in a colander.

Rice, Lentils & Veggies

Leslie Margiatto
Lawrenceville, NJ

This recipe has been passed between friends for a long time.

1 T. oil
1 c. carrots, peeled and sliced
2 to 3 stalks celery, chopped
1 onion, chopped
1 c. long-cooking rice, uncooked
1 c. dried lentils, rinsed
2 10-3/4 oz. cans vegetable
   broth
15-oz. can black beans

1/2 t. dried oregano
1/2 t. dried basil
2 cloves garlic, chopped
pepper to taste
2 T. catsup
2 14-1/2 oz. cans stewed
   tomatoes
10-oz. pkg. frozen spinach,
   thawed and drained

Heat oil in a skillet; add carrots, celery, onion, rice and lentils. Cook for 5 to 7 minutes; stir in remaining ingredients. Cover; simmer for 30 to 45 minutes or until vegetables are tender. Serves 8 to 10.

Float lemon and lime slices along with a few sliced strawberries in a pitcher of icy water to make it taste and look anything but ordinary!

very Veggie Sides & Salads

Homestyle Cheesy Veggies

Jen Sell
Farmington, MO

This is a yummy addition to any meal and so easy to prepare.

2 16-oz. pkgs. frozen mixed
  vegetables
10-3/4 oz. can cream of
  mushroom soup
8-oz. pasteurized processed
  cheese spread, cubed

8-oz. can sliced water chestnuts,
  drained
salt and pepper to taste

Cook vegetables according to package directions; set aside. Heat soup
and cheese together until cheese melts; spoon into a 2-quart casserole
dish. Mix in vegetables, water chestnuts, salt and pepper; bake at
350 degrees for 20 to 30 minutes. Serves 10 to 12.

*Hang a steel washboard
where messages,
calendars and to-do lists
can easily be found. The
steel board means
magnets will hold and
corral notes easily!*

Roasted Pepper Potato Topper

Jo Ann

With a prep time of only 5 minutes, this is a must-try recipe!
Spooned onto a big baked potato, it's terrific!

8-oz. container sour cream
7-oz. jar roasted red peppers,
   drained
8-oz. pkg. cream cheese,
   softened and divided

1 clove garlic, minced
1 T. fresh basil, chopped
1/2 t. dried oregano

Blend together sour cream, red peppers and half the cream cheese.
Reserve remaining cream cheese for another recipe. Stir in garlic, basil
and oregano until well blended. Chill one hour. Makes about 5 cups.

Set out all the fixin's for a spud-tacular potato bar for
dinner tonight! Let the kids set out their favorite
toppers...a fun way to get everyone involved.

Hot
Off *the* Grill

Grilling tips to get fired up over!

✦ Buy skinless chicken or turkey to reduce calories. If you're worried about the meat drying out while cooking, rub on a layer of mayonnaise. It seals in the juices to keep the meat moist while cooking, but isn't absorbed.

✦ Before cooking on the grill brush the rack with vegetable oil or use a non-stick vegetable spray before heating the grill. This keeps the foods from sticking and makes cleanup easier too.

✦ For fuss-free grilled vegetables lay them in heavy-duty aluminum foil, dot with butter and seal the foil. Place the package on the grill for a few minutes just until they're tender.

✦ Tossing whole potatoes on the grill? They take a long time to heat up so be sure to give them at least 30 minutes.

✦ Remember that whenever you're barbecuing, use tongs or a spatula to turn the meat not a fork. A fork will let the natural juices to escape, causing meat to become tough.

Hot Off the Grill

Good-for-You Grilled Salmon

Phyl Broich-Wessling
Garner, IA

Salmon grills in no time...give it a try!

2 lbs. salmon fillets, skin on
1 t. coriander seed
1 t. cumin seed
1 t. mustard seed
1/4 t. salt

1/4 t. peppercorns
1-1/2 t. paprika
1 T. brown sugar, packed
2 T. olive oil

Rinse salmon and set aside. In a small skillet, toast coriander seed, cumin seed and mustard seed over medium-high heat for 2 minutes, stirring often. Remove from heat and stir in salt, peppercorns and paprika; let cool slightly. Transfer to a blender and blend until finely ground. Pour into a bowl and stir in brown sugar. Brush fillets with olive oil; then rub spice mixture onto non-skin side of fillets. Cover and refrigerate one to 2 hours. For charcoal grill, grill fish skin-side down over medium coals just until fish begins to flake easily, about 4 to 6 minutes per 1/2-inch thickness of fillets. For a gas grill, cover and grill over medium heat until fish begins to flake easily. Remove and discard skin before serving. Serves 8.

To keep seafood from sticking to the grill, slice a raw potato in half lengthwise. Once the grill is hot, slide the cut potato down the grill in one direction. The starch from the potato will coat the grill and make it non-stick!

Dijon Grilled Fish

Bonnie Weatherford
Aurora, IN

Serve alongside a crispy salad and you've got a really terrific meal.

1/2 c. margarine
2 T. Dijon mustard
1 t. seasoned salt

2 T. lemon juice
1 lb. orange roughy fillets
paprika to taste

Combine margarine, mustard, salt and lemon juice in a saucepan; simmer for 10 minutes. Let cool; pour over fish. Cover and marinate for 30 minutes. Grill over medium coals for 3 to 6 minutes on each side, using remaining sauce for basting. Sprinkle with paprika. Serves 2 to 4.

Always keep fresh lemon juice and some melted butter handy while you are grilling fish. Just brushing them on while grilling helps keep the fish moist.

Hot Off the Grill

Marinated Flank Steak

Irene Robinson
Cincinnati, OH

Refrigerating the steaks in a spicy marinade really adds to the flavor.

1 to 2 beef flank steaks
1/2 c. soy sauce
2 T. honey
2 T. white vinegar
1-1/2 T. ground ginger

1-1/2 t. garlic powder
1-1/2 t. cinnamon
1-1/2 t. nutmeg
3/4 c. oil
1 onion, chopped

Using a sharp knife, make shallow cuts in steaks; set aside. Mix remaining ingredients together in a large plastic zipping bag; add steaks. Refrigerate for at least 24 hours, turning several times. Grill or broil for 5 to 10 minutes on each side. Slice thinly on an angle to serve. Serves 2 to 4.

A great way to prepare meals ahead of time...wrap meats and vegetables up in foil packets. When dinnertime rolls around, just cook them quickly and easily on the grill.

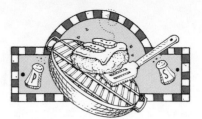

Citrus Grill

Robyn Wright
Delaware, OH

A yummy marinated chicken recipe from a friend on Prince Edwards Island.

1/4 c. oil
1/4 c. orange juice
1/4 c. tarragon red wine vinegar
1 t. dried basil
1 t. dried oregano

1 T. grated Parmesan cheese
2 t. Dijon mustard
1/4 t. garlic, pressed
8 to 12 boneless, skinless
  chicken breasts

Mix all ingredients except chicken in a jar; cover and shake well. Place chicken breasts in a large plastic zipping bag. Pour marinade over chicken, seal bag and refrigerate for at least 2 hours, turning bag occasionally. Arrange chicken on heated grill and cook 7 to 10 minutes on each side, turning only once, until juices run clear. Makes 8 to 12 servings.

A gift for Dad of a spatula, tongs and a basting brush would be terrific tucked inside an oven mitt!

Hot Off the Grill

Herb-Grilled Steak

Carla Pindell
Hilliard, OH

Sauté mushrooms and onions to serve on each steak...a must-have along with a big baked potato!

3 to 4-lb. beef sirloin or
    porterhouse steak, 1 to
    1-1/2 inches thick
1 t. onion salt
1/2 c. vinegar

1/4 c. oil
1/4 t. dried thyme
1/4 t. dried tarragon
1/4 t. dried dill weed
1/4 t. dried sage

Rub both sides of steak with onion salt; place in a shallow container and set aside. Combine remaining ingredients and pour over steak. Marinate at least one hour, turning occasionally. Grill or broil steak about 6 inches from heat, 15 to 20 minutes on each side, brushing frequently with herb marinade. Serves 6 to 8.

Remember spices can be sprinkled on food up to one hour before grilling...this really lets the meat or seafood absorb the flavors.

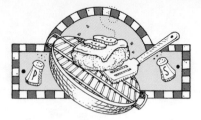

Lemon Barbecued Chicken

Lori Slyh
Galloway, OH

A real tangy twist from traditional barbecued chicken.

2-1/2 to 3 lbs. boneless, skinless
  chicken breasts
1 c. oil
3/4 c. lemon juice
1 T. seasoned salt

2 t. paprika
2 t. onion powder
2 t. dried basil
2 t. dried thyme
1/2 t. garlic powder

Place chicken in a shallow pan; set aside. Combine remaining
ingredients in a jar; cover and shake to blend. Pour over chicken;
cover. Refrigerate several hours or overnight, turning occasionally.
Grill chicken over hot coals 15 to 20 minutes, turning frequently, until
juices run clear, basting often with marinade. Serves 4 to 6.

Try layering vegetables and meat for tasty kabobs.
Just remember when using wooden skewers, they need
to be soaked in water for at least 30 minutes before
grilling to prevent them from burning.

Hot Off the Grill

Kentucky Wildcat Chicken

Claire Bertram
Lexington, KY

To keep the toothpicks from burning, soak them in water for 10 minutes before adding chicken.

1/2 c. teriyaki basting & glazing sauce
2 T. bourbon or chicken broth
2 T. honey
2 t. mustard
1/4 t. pepper
4 boneless, skinless chicken breasts
4 slices bacon

Combine teriyaki sauce, bourbon or broth, honey, mustard and pepper. Brush mixture evenly over chicken. Roll up chicken and wrap with bacon slices; secure with toothpicks. Grill over medium-hot coals for 15 to 20 minutes, turning and basting frequently, until juices run clear. Serves 4.

Layer colorful bandannas over picnic tables to give them a splash of color!

Tropical Chicken

Wendy Lee Paffenroth
Pine Island, NY

You can also make this ahead of time and refrigerate. Just heat through before serving.

5 to 6 boneless, skinless chicken
    breasts
1/2 to 3/4 c. water
2 onions, sliced
1 green pepper, sliced

3/4 to 1 c. sweet & sour
    duck sauce
20-oz. can pineapple chunks
1/4 c. brown sugar, packed
1/8 t. cornstarch

Grill chicken for 15 to 20 minutes until juices run clear; set aside. Place water, onions and pepper in a skillet; cook over low heat until tender. Stir in pineapple; bring to a boil. Pour in duck sauce; stir until well blended. Add brown sugar and cornstarch; mix well. Add chicken to skillet and simmer until heated through. Serves 4.

Looking for a simple appetizer while waiting for the food to grill? Brush grilled bread with olive oil and top with feta cheese...delicious!

Barbecued Cheeseburgers

*Tamara Wallace
Roscoe, IL*

*My sister-in-law gave me the recipe for these great cheeseburgers.
We like to make them at backyard cookouts...burgers never
tasted so good!*

2 lbs. ground beef
2 T. dried, minced onion
2 t. Worcestershire sauce
2 t. mustard
1 t. salt

1-1/2 t. pepper
1-1/2 c. sharp Cheddar cheese,
   shredded
Optional: melted garlic butter,
   5 hamburger buns

Thoroughly mix together ground beef, onions, Worcestershire sauce,
mustard, salt and pepper. Shape into 10 thin patties. Place
approximately 1/4 cup cheese on top of 5 patties; top each with
another patty and press together to seal. Grill over hot coals to desired
doneness. For extra flavor, brush with melted garlic butter during
grilling. Serve alone or on toasted buns. Makes 5 servings.

*Tote a grill to the beach for a
terrific seaside barbecue!*

Summertime Potatoes

Marianne Terry
Elma, NY

You could also put all the ingredients in a foil pouch and toss on the grill...so simple!

6 to 8 potatoes, cubed
1/2 to 3/4 lb. bacon, crisply
   cooked and crumbled
1 green pepper, chopped

1 bunch green onions, sliced
8-oz. pkg. shredded Cheddar
   cheese
salt and pepper to taste

Mix all ingredients together in a foil pan. Cover with aluminum foil; grill until potatoes are tender, about 20 minutes. Serves 6 to 8.

Not enough seating at the patio table? Spread blankets on the grass and serve dinner picnic-style...the kids will love it!

Hot Off the Grill

Zesty Grilled Pork Chops

Irene Robinson
Cincinnati, OH

This is the only way my family wants to grill pork chops!

3/4 c. soy sauce
1/4 c. lemon juice
1 T. chili sauce

1 T. brown sugar, packed
1/4 t. garlic powder
6 pork chops

Combine the first 5 ingredients in a large plastic zipping bag; mix well. Reserve and refrigerate 1/4 cup of mixture for basting. Place pork chops in bag; shake to coat. Refrigerate 3 hours or overnight. Drain and discard marinade. Grill chops, covered, for 4 minutes; turn and baste with reserved mixture. Grill for 4 to 7 minutes or until juices run clear. Serves 6.

*Keep the atmosphere fun when grilling in the evening.
Pull out tiki torches, set candles in hurricane lanterns
and hang strands of twinkly white lights.*

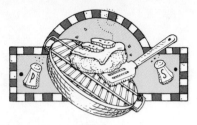

Crunchy Chicken Burgers

Laura Koppelmann
Kissimmee, FL

A delicious burger with a twist!

1 lb. ground chicken
1/4 c. honey barbecue sauce
3/4 c. mini shredded wheat
   cereal, crushed

1 egg, beaten
1/8 t. salt
1/8 t. pepper

Mix all ingredients together; form into patties. Grill until cooked through. Serves 4 to 6.

Fill a whitewashed wire basket with several clay pots...ideal for holding silverware, napkins, condiments or pretty posies.

ᴴᵒᵗ Off the Grill

Red-Hot Pork Chops

Janice Maas
Janesville, MN

Add even more cayenne and red pepper flakes for extra heat!

1/2 c. orange juice
3 T. brown sugar, packed
1 T. lemon-garlic seasoning
1/4 t. cayenne pepper

1/2 t. red pepper flakes
1 T. oil
4 boneless pork chops

Combine the first 6 ingredients in a plastic zipping bag; add pork chops. Refrigerate for at least 30 minutes, up to 12 hours. Remove meat from marinade; discard marinade. Grill for 7 to 9 minutes per side or until cooked through. Serves 4.

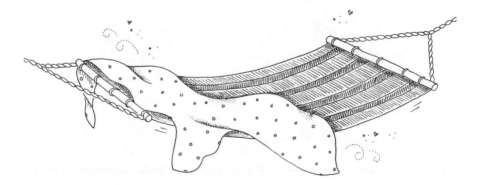

Grilling means summertime fun...pick up some squirt guns or small battery-operated fans to keep everyone cool.

Garlic Ranch Chicken

Joy Diomede
Double Oaks, TX

Serve with cool ranch salad dressing for dipping.

1 c. ranch salad dressing
2 T. garlic, chopped
1 T. fresh basil, minced

4 to 6 boneless, skinless chicken
    breasts

Combine dressing, garlic and basil in a large plastic zipping bag. Add chicken; turn to coat. Squeeze out excess air; seal bag. Refrigerate up to 24 hours until ready to grill. Grill chicken for 15 to 20 minutes until juices run clear when pierced. Makes 4 to 6 servings.

Keep the picnic tablecloth in place by attaching small tablecloth weights to the edges. Many department stores carry them, or make your own by stitching on a few heavy beads or even fishing sinkers to do the same job.

Bestest Burger Ever

Carol Daugherty
Lexington, OH

I think you'll agree, it is the best!

2 lbs. ground beef
1 onion, chopped
1 t. salt
1 t. pepper
1 t. dried basil
1/3 c. teriyaki sauce

1/4 c. Italian seasoned bread
crumbs
1 T. grated Parmesan cheese
6 slices American cheese
6 onion rolls

Mix together beef, onion, salt, pepper and basil. Add teriyaki sauce, bread crumbs and Parmesan cheese; mix well. Divide into 6 patties. Grill to desired doneness; top with American cheese. Serve on onion rolls. Makes 6 sandwiches.

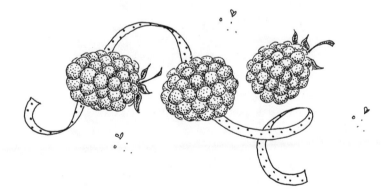

Keep those pesky pests away naturally...set terra cotta pots filled with mint plants around the picnic table and grilling area.

Honeyed Broilers

Carrie Obry
Oak Park, IL

When I want to dress up dinner a little, I arrange the grilled chicken on a bed of mixed greens.

2-1/2 to 3 lb. chicken, quartered
4 cloves garlic, minced
1-1/2 t. dried marjoram
1 t. dry mustard
1/4 t. salt
1/4 t. pepper
2 T. honey
2 T. balsamic vinegar

Remove skin from chicken quarters, if desired; arrange in a casserole dish. Mix garlic, marjoram, mustard, salt and pepper; rub into chicken. Combine honey and vinegar; brush over chicken. Cover and refrigerate for at least 2 hours. Place chicken, bone-side down, over medium heat on grill rack above drip pan. Cover; grill for 50 minutes to one hour, until chicken juices run clear. Makes 4 servings.

An insulated cooler with a fitted lid works great for holding warm water to quickly wash up with after cooking outdoors. Great for wiping little chins covered in barbecue sauce too!

Hot Off the Grill

Teriyaki Grilled Vegetables

Nancy Molldrem
Eau Claire, WI

The best-tasting side dish ever!

16-oz. can whole potatoes, drained and halved
8-oz. pkg. cherry tomatoes
8-oz. pkg. mushrooms
1 bunch green onions, cut into 2-inch lengths
20-oz. can pineapple tidbits, drained
1 green pepper, cut into strips
1 red pepper, cut into strips
1 yellow squash, peeled and sliced
10-oz. bottle teriyaki marinade

Combine vegetables and fruit in a large bowl; toss with teriyaki marinade and let stand for 15 minutes. Arrange in a grill wok and place on grill; stir occasionally for 10 to 15 minutes until hot and golden. Makes 4 to 6 servings.

Leftovers are no problem...turn grilled vegetables into a delicious salad by serving over mixed salad greens and drizzling with balsamic vinegar or any favorite salad dressing.

Honey Marinade

Trish Menzia
Boulder Junction, WI

A great marinade for any kind of meat...just refrigerate several hours or overnight. It's especially good for pork. Paired with a fresh salad and sweet corn, it's my family's favorite summer meal!

1/2 c. soy sauce
1/2 c. honey
1/2 c. water
1/4 c. beer or beef broth
2 T. sugar

1 t. ground ginger
2 t. garlic, chopped
1 t. mustard
1 t. salt
1/4 t. pepper

Combine all ingredients; mix well. Makes about 1-3/4 cups.

Outdoor parties can have a whimsical theme to make decorating more fun! Choose something easy that everyone will enjoy...a beach party, fiesta or western barbecue would all be terrific.

Steak Sauce

Doris Stegner
Gooseberry Patch

A savory steak sauce recipe I use whenever we have company.

1 c. sliced mushrooms
2 T. fresh chives, chopped
2 T. slivered almonds, toasted
2 T. butter

1/3 c. white wine or chicken
   broth
1/4 t. salt
1/8 t. fines herbes

Sauté mushrooms, chives and almonds with butter in a skillet until mushrooms and chives are tender. Stir in wine or broth, salt and fines herbes. Heat through; do not boil. Serve over grilled steak. Makes about 1-2/3 cups.

Bring the Lazy Susan out of the kitchen and put it on the picnic table...so easy for guests to reach the sauces, condiments and seasonings they need.

Simply the Best Barbecue Sauce

Bonnie Astuto
Dingmans Ferry, PA

This recipe is quick, easy and great tasting! I usually double the recipe so there's extra sauce at the table for dipping. I use it for barbecued ribs or chicken and even broiled or baked chicken too.

1/4 c. molasses
1/3 c. catsup
1 T. lemon juice

2 t. dry mustard
1/4 t. chili powder
1/8 t. garlic powder

Combine all ingredients; mix well. Brush over ribs or chicken; grill. Makes about 3/4 cup.

A welcome hostess gift...give a variety of barbecue sauces, marinades and rubs in a painted pail. Guests will love trying them out during the get-together.

Hot Off the Grill

Best-Ever Grilled Flank Steak

Bonnie Weber
West Palm Beach, FL

A hint of lime gives this steak its extra-special flavor.

1 to 1-1/2 lb. beef flank steak
10-oz. can beef consommé
1 c. red wine or beef broth
2/3 c. soy sauce

4 cloves garlic, minced
1 T. lime juice
1 T. brown sugar, packed

Using a sharp knife, make shallow cuts in meat on each side in 1-1/2 inch squares; place in a shallow pan. Combine remaining ingredients; mix well. Pour over steak; cover and refrigerate for 8 hours, turning occasionally. Drain steak, reserving marinade. Grill over medium heat for 7 to 9 minutes on each side until steak reaches desired doneness, basting twice with marinade. To serve, slice across grain. Serves 6.

Terra-cotta pots make a table setting shine. Use silver acrylic paint to coat the insides and top rims of 3-inch pots, allow to dry and place votives inside.

Stop-You-in-Your-Tracks Grilled Salsa

Zoe Groff
Lebanon, TN

You'll never buy store bought again...we don't! This salsa is a must-have at all family gatherings. I've been known to quadruple the recipe and share with friends.

10 roma tomatoes, divided
8 jalapeños, divided
1/2 bunch fresh cilantro, minced
1 onion, chopped

6 to 10 cloves garlic, minced
1-1/2 T. lemon juice
1 T. lime juice
salt and pepper to taste

Combine 5 tomatoes and 4 jalapeños in a saucepan; cover with water and simmer for 25 minutes. Arrange remaining tomatoes and jalapeños on grill; heat until tender and slightly blackened. Remove stems from jalapeños; cut into chunks. Combine tomatoes, jalapeños and remaining ingredients in a blender; blend to desired consistency, about 30 to 40 seconds. Chill and serve. Makes 3 to 4 cups.

The grill's heating up and the neighbors are gathered around the picnic table. Be sure to keep softball gear or a deck of cards on hand for lots of old-fashioned fun while everyone's together.

Rosemary-Lemon Pork Chops

Joy Diomede
Double Oaks, TX

This recipe comes from my Mom & Dad...both excellent cooks!

4 cloves garlic, minced
1/2 lemon
1/4 c. olive oil

1 T. fresh rosemary, minced
4 pork chops

Combine all ingredients except pork chops in a large plastic zipping bag; mix well. Add pork chops and turn to coat. Refrigerate 8 hours, turning occasionally; discard marinade. Grill until cooked through. Makes 4 servings.

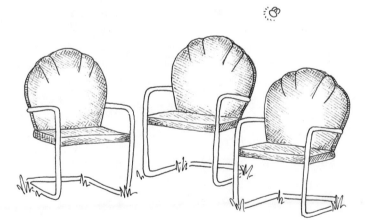

Vintage shell-back lawn chairs are ideal for outdoor gatherings... pick some up at the next flea market. They have just enough spring to be comfortable so adults can enjoy a long chat while the kids run around catching fireflies.

Tangy Brown Sugar Ham

Alyce Leitzel
Hegins, PA

Thick slices of ham with a sweet-hot sauce.

1 c. brown sugar, packed
1/3 c. prepared horseradish

1/4 c. lemon juice
4 slices ham, cut 1-inch thick

Combine sugar, horseradish and lemon juice in a saucepan; bring to a boil. Brush over ham; grill over high heat for 6 to 8 minutes on each side until heated through. Serves 4.

Try grilling veggies on rosemary skewers for a delicious change. To make the skewers, pull off all but the top leaves from the stem and whittle the opposite end into a point. Slide on vegetables and grill...yummy!

Hot Off the Grill

Grilled Garlic-Stuffed Steaks

Tricia Schreier
San Jose, CA

Perfect paired with baked potatoes and steamed asparagus.

1 T. olive oil
1/4 c. garlic, chopped
1/2 c. green onion, chopped

1/4 t. pepper
2 boneless beef top loin steaks,
    cut 2 inches thick

Heat oil in a skillet; add garlic and sauté for 4 to 5 minutes or until tender. Sprinkle in onion; continue to cook for 4 to 5 more minutes until tender. Sprinkle with pepper and set aside. Cut a pocket in each steak; start 1/2 inch from one long side of steak and cut horizontally through the center of the steak to within 1/2 inch of other side. Spread half of garlic mixture inside each steak pocket; secure opening with a metal skewer. Grill, covered, for 22 to 24 minutes or to desired doneness, turning occasionally. Slice steaks crosswise 1/2-inch thick. Serves 6.

Tie up a bunch of fragrant herbs with jute or raffia to use as a basting brush while grilling.

A-Little-Ginger Beef Marinade

Connie Spangler
Palm Bay, FL

I first tasted beef marinated with this recipe at my sister-in-law's home. She's an excellent cook, and from the first bite, my family declared this recipe a keeper.

3/4 c. soy sauce
1/4 c. white vinegar
1/4 c. brown sugar, packed

3 T. Worcestershire sauce
2 T. oil
1 t. ground ginger

Combine all ingredients in a jar; cover and refrigerate until ready to grill. When ready to use, place meat in a large plastic zipping bag and top with marinade. Refrigerate 24 hours, turning occasionally. Grill meat as desired. Makes about 1-1/2 cups.

Garlic, Salt & Paprika Rub

Reivan Zeleznik
Stamford, CT

An ideal rub for brisket, beef, turkey, chicken or roasted potatoes.

26-oz. box salt
1 whole bulb garlic, peeled

3 to 4 T. paprika, divided

Pour salt into a large mixing bowl. Press garlic directly into salt so all of the liquid is added to the rub. Do not mash. Add paprika by the spoonfuls until mixture is a medium brown color, mixing between spoonfuls. Store in a tightly covered container. To use, rub on brisket, roast beef, turkey, chicken, roasted potatoes or vegetables and refrigerate for 1 to 2 days. Makes one pint.

Dinner *for* Two

Cooking for two, or just you.

✴ Smaller appliances such as toaster ovens, mini food processors and slow cookers hold just the right amount of food for two.

✴ Don't forget that eggs can be bought by the half dozen too.

✴ Did you know you can use broth for just as much flavor and less fat when making mashed potatoes? Creamy and oh-so delicious even without adding milk!

✴ Use sugar substitutes whenever you can...
they're twice as sweet and have only one or 2 calories, while sugar is 30 calories per teaspoon!

✴ Slow cookers come in many sizes...the smallest holds about 3 cups. Just right for small serving sauces, dips or spreads.

✴ Pick up some mini loaf pans...they're ideal for bread, quick bread or meatloaf.

✴ Stock up on the single-serving size cans of vegetables and soups...they're just the right size.

Dinner *for* Two

Tangy Stroganoff

Stella Hickman
Gooseberry Patch

A tasty dinner that can't be beat.

16-oz. pkg. sliced mushrooms
1 onion, chopped
2 T. olive oil
1-1/2 lbs. roast beef, cubed
12-oz. container onion chip dip

1 T. tomato paste
1/4 c. sherry or apple juice
salt and pepper to taste
8-oz. pkg. egg noodles, cooked

Sauté mushrooms and onion in oil in a large skillet for 5 minutes until tender. Add meat, olive oil, dip and tomato paste; mix well. Stir in sherry or juice; simmer over low heat for 3 to 4 minutes, stirring frequently. Add salt and pepper to taste; serve over prepared noodles. Makes 2 servings.

If a recipe serves 4 or 5 and you find you have
leftovers, no problem...they're great for next-day
meals. Soups, stews and casseroles make quick & easy
lunches, or freeze leftovers for a heat-and-serve meal
later when time is short.

Baked Chicken & Potatoes

Vickie

A delicious combination.

2 boneless, skinless chicken
  breasts
2 T. Dijon mustard, divided
1/2 c. biscuit baking mix
3/4 lb. redskin potatoes,
  quartered

1 red or green pepper, cut into
  strips
1 onion, cut into wedges
Optional: 2 T. grated Parmesan
  cheese
1/2 t. paprika

Brush chicken with one tablespoon mustard; coat with baking mix. Arrange chicken breasts in corners of a 13"x9" baking dish sprayed with non-stick vegetable spray. Place vegetables in center of dish; brush with remaining mustard. Sprinkle evenly with cheese and paprika. Bake 35 to 40 minutes at 400 degrees, stirring vegetables after 20 minutes, until potatoes are tender and juices of chicken run clear when pierced. Makes 2 servings.

Look for frozen vegetables and substitute them for fresh when cooking for two. Cook only what you need for one meal and return the rest to the freezer.

Dinner for Two

Beef & Mushroom Casserole

Donna Cash
Dexter, MI

I think this is the best ever low-carb casserole...you'll never miss the pasta.

1/2 lb. ground beef, browned
1-1/2 T. olive oil
3 stalks celery, chopped
2 carrots, chopped
4-oz. can sliced mushrooms,
   drained

1 onion, quartered
1 T. garlic, minced
1 t. Italian seasoning
1/8 t. cayenne pepper
salt and pepper to taste

Brown ground beef in a skillet; drain. Remove from skillet and set aside. Heat oil over medium heat in a skillet; add celery and carrots and continue heating for 5 minutes. Add remaining ingredients except ground beef; mix well. Cover and simmer about 5 minutes on medium until all vegetables are tender. Add ground beef and stir until heated through, about 5 minutes. Makes 2 servings.

Don't forget to take advantage of the salad bar in the local supermarket. It's a great idea to buy smaller portions of already prepared and chopped vegetables to use in stir-fries, casseroles and salads.

Lemon & Artichoke Chicken

Karen Lee Puchnick
Lyndora, PA

*After enjoying a similar dish at a restaurant, I created
my own version that is just as tasty!*

2 boneless, skinless chicken
   breasts
3 T. all-purpose flour, divided
2 T. butter
1/2 c. white wine or chicken
   broth

2 cloves garlic, minced
1/3 c. lemon juice
1/2 c. chicken broth
4 artichoke hearts, quartered
4-oz. can sliced mushrooms,
   drained

Pound chicken breasts flat; lightly coat each with one teaspoon flour.
Sauté in butter until golden, about 5 minutes. Remove chicken; stir
enough remaining flour into skillet to thicken. Add wine or broth,
garlic, lemon juice and chicken broth; stir over low heat until sauce is
smooth. Return chicken to skillet; add artichokes and mushrooms.
Simmer, covered, 8 to 10 minutes until juices from chicken run clear.
Serves 2.

Sometimes even when a small roast or chicken is
prepared, there will be leftovers. Set them aside for
sandwiches or as tasty salad toppers, then put the
rest into a plastic freezer bag to use in another recipe.

Dinner *for* Two

Linguine with Garlic Sauce

Connie Bryant
Topeka, KS

*This is a wonderful dish that's easy to make and is perfect
for a weeknight dinner.*

3 T. butter
8-oz. pkg. sliced mushrooms
3 cloves garlic, minced
1/2 t. dried rosemary
1/4 t. pepper
1/2 c. whipping cream

salt to taste
8-oz. pkg. linguine, uncooked
   and divided
1 c. shredded mozzarella cheese
Garnish: fresh chopped parsley

Melt butter in heavy skillet over medium heat; add mushrooms, garlic,
rosemary and pepper. Sauté about 5 minutes until mushrooms release
their juices, stirring occasionally. Stir in cream; simmer until mixture
thickens slightly, about 3 minutes. Add salt to taste. Prepare half of
the linguine according to package directions; use the remaining
linguine in another recipe. Add prepared linguine and cheese to skillet;
stir until cheese melts. Sprinkle with parsley. Makes 2 servings.

*When my mother had to get dinner for eight, she'd just
make enough for 16 and only serve half.*

-Gracie Allen

Surf & Turf

Janet Myers
Reading, PA

This recipe is one I know I can count on, and do for special occasions.

2 T. butter
1/4 t. garlic powder
2 4-oz. filet mignon steaks
1.8-oz. pkg. onion soup mix
1/3 c. water

2 T. dry red wine or beef broth
1 T. fresh parsley, minced
6 raw shrimp, peeled and
   cleaned

Melt butter with garlic powder in a skillet. Add steaks; sauté over medium heat for 2 minutes on each side. Combine soup mix, water, wine or broth and parsley; mix well and pour into skillet. Add shrimp. Simmer, uncovered, turning shrimp and steaks once, for 4 minutes or until cooked to desired doneness. Serves 2.

Take advantage of the cut-to-order meat counter.
Purchase meats, poultry and seafood in any amount
needed...just ask to have your purchases packaged in
2-serving portions, such as 2 pork chops or
8 ounces of ground meat.

⋆ Dinner for Two

Easy Beef & Mushrooms

Teresa Sullivan
Westerville, OH

A favorite meal spooned over homemade mashed potatoes.

1 lb. ground beef
1/2 c. onion, chopped
1 clove garlic, minced
8-oz. pkg. sliced mushrooms
1 T. butter
2 T. all-purpose flour
1/4 t. pepper
1/2 t. salt
1/4 t. paprika
1/2 c. chicken broth
10-3/4 oz. can cream of chicken
    soup
1 c. sour cream
1-1/2 c. prepared mashed
    potatoes

Sauté beef, onion, garlic and mushrooms in butter in a large skillet; drain well. Sprinkle flour and seasonings over meat mixture; stir well. Add remaining ingredients except potatoes; mix well and simmer about 30 minutes. Watch carefully to prevent scorching. Serve over potatoes. Makes 2 servings.

Think about starting a cooking club with friends...a great way to swap recipes! Cook larger casseroles and then simply divide them up for each other person in the group. Everyone gets to sample something new and have fun all at the same time.

Chicken in Cream Sauce

Carol Holtman
Colorado Springs, CO

Of all my favorite recipes, this one is very simple and elegant. I serve it with rice, steamed vegetables and pineapple spears.

2 T. butter
2 boneless, skinless chicken
    breasts
1/2 onion, chopped

1-1/2 c. whipping cream
1 egg yolk
1 T. lemon juice

Melt butter in a heavy pan; sauté chicken and onion for about 40 minutes. Stir in cream; reduce heat and simmer for 7 to 10 minutes. Remove chicken and keep warm on serving dish. Beat egg yolk and lemon juice into the sauce and let thicken. Pour over chicken. Makes 2 servings.

Bags of salad mix are real time-savers. Keep opened bags of greens crispy by storing in airtight containers or plastic zipping bags...just be sure to squeeze out all the air before refrigerating.

Dinner for Two

Country-Style Meatloaf

Jacque Coppock
Worthington, IN

Don't forget all the good things that go with this...mashed potatoes, fresh vegetables and warm rolls. Yum!

1 lb. ground beef
1 T. dried, minced onion
1 t. salt
1/2 t. pepper
1 egg

1/4 c. dry bread crumbs
15-oz. can tomato sauce, divided
2 t. Worcestershire sauce
1 t. fresh parsley, chopped
1 T. brown sugar, packed

Mix together ground beef, onion, salt, pepper, egg, bread crumbs and half of tomato sauce. Form into 2 small loaves; place in an 11"x8" baking pan and bake at 425 degrees for 20 minutes. Mix together remaining tomato sauce, Worcestershire sauce, parsley and brown sugar. Spread mixture over meat loaves and bake for 5 minutes longer. Let cool 5 minutes. Serves 2.

Dividing canned foods into recipes for 2 is a snap. Shop for the size of can specified in the recipe, and if less than a whole can of tomato sauce, broth, or spaghetti sauce is used, refrigerate the remainder in an airtight container for a few days, or freeze it for up to 3 months.

Peppered Steak

Dale Duncan
Waterloo, LA

Ready in less than 10 minutes!

2 t. lemon-pepper seasoning
1-lb. beef sirloin steak
1/2 T. butter

1/8 c. brandy or apple juice
1/8 c. beef bouillon granules
Garnish: fresh parsley

Rub seasoning over both sides of steak, pressing into meat surface. Melt butter in large heavy skillet. Sauté steak over medium-high heat, 5 to 7 minutes on each side or to desired doneness. Remove steak to platter; keep warm. Stir brandy or juice and bouillon into skillet. Bring to a boil and simmer 2 minutes. Pour over steak. Sprinkle with parsley. Serves 2.

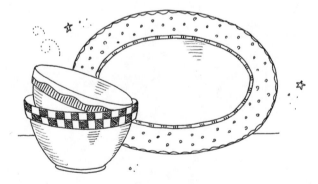

They hadn't learned how to cook for 2, either, so this feast was enough for 40, and they were pretty sure they'd be eating leftover turkey and stuffing until the 4th of July!

Rev. Sarah Lammert

Dinner *for* Two

Patchwork Pasta

Valerie Bishop
Fairchild AFB, WA

So colorful!

3 boneless, skinless chicken
   breasts, cubed
2 T. olive oil, divided
lemon-pepper seasoning to taste
1 green pepper, chopped

1 yellow pepper, chopped
1 orange pepper, chopped
1 onion, chopped
14-1/2 oz. can diced tomatoes
2 to 4 c. prepared linguini

Sauté chicken in one tablespoon oil in a skillet until juices run clear.
Sprinkle with seasoning; remove from skillet and set aside. Sauté
peppers and onion in remaining oil until tender. Add chicken and
tomatoes; heat through. Serve over prepared linguine. Makes
2 servings.

Spend an afternoon creating a memory box with a
dear friend. Add all those trinkets that make your
friendship special...ticket stubs, photos, game pieces,
buttons or seashells. A heartfelt keepsake shared
between best friends.

Sauerkraut & Pork Chops

Mary Hageny
Rhinelander, WI

A well-loved recipe from my mother.

2 pork chops
1 T. oil
8-oz. pkg. egg noodles,
  uncooked

16-oz. can sauerkraut, drained
  and rinsed
1 c. chicken broth

Brown pork chops in oil in a roaster; remove and set aside. Prepare noodles as directed on package for only half the suggested cooking time. Place in the bottom of roaster; arrange pork chops over noodles and top with sauerkraut. Add chicken broth and enough water to cover bottom of roaster. Bake at 325 degrees for one hour or until meat is tender. Makes 2 servings.

Jot down all your favorite, tried & true recipes for the new bride who's just learning to cook for 2. She'll love 'em!

⁕ Dinner *for* Two

Sweet-Tart Cranberry Chicken

Suzan Detwiler
Easton, PA

This is the first recipe my best friend and I exchanged years ago.
She has since moved quite a distance away, but whenever
I serve this, I feel like she's right next to me.

2 boneless, skinless chicken
   breasts
1/2 c. onion, chopped
1 T. oil

1 c. catsup
1/2 c. brown sugar, packed
2 to 3 t. orange zest
1 c. cranberries

Bake chicken, uncovered, in a greased 13"x9" pan at 400 degrees for
25 minutes. Sauté onions in oil over medium heat; add catsup, brown
sugar, orange zest and cranberries. Pour over chicken breasts and
bake, uncovered, an additional 20 minutes. Makes 2 servings.

In late summer, divide some favorite perennial
flowers and share them with a dear friend...the
beginning of a delightful friendship garden.

Lemon Chicken

Julie Milliken
Gooseberry Patch

The lemon curd is what makes this recipe special. I like to add steamed rice and a tossed salad alongside when serving.

1/4 c. all-purpose flour	1/2 c. chicken broth
1/8 t. salt	1/4 c. hot water
1-1/2 lbs. boneless, skinless	10-oz. jar lemon curd
chicken breast, cubed	1/4 c. fresh chives, chopped
2 T. oil	1 T. lemon zest

Blend flour and salt in a shallow dish; coat chicken lightly. Heat oil in a large skillet over medium heat; add chicken. Cook and stir until golden, 3 to 4 minutes. Remove chicken from pan and set aside. Reduce heat to medium; add broth to pan, using a fork to mix well. Stir hot water into lemon curd; whisk curd into broth in skillet. Return chicken to pan; simmer one to 2 minutes until sauce thickens and chicken is cooked through. Remove pan from heat. Add chives and lemon zest; mix well. Makes 2 servings.

What's the nicest gift for 2 brand-new parents? A dinner delivered straight to their door!

Dinner for Two

3-Cheese Spinach Lasagna

Lynn Williams
Muncie, IN

Sometimes I add a dash of cinnamon with the ricotta mixture.

1 onion, chopped
1 t. garlic, minced
1 T. oil
10-oz. pkg. frozen spinach,
   thawed and drained
1 egg, beaten
1 c. ricotta cheese

1/4 c. grated Parmesan cheese
3/4 c. shredded mozzarella
   cheese, divided
4 strips no-boil lasagna,
   uncooked
1 c. spaghetti sauce, divided

Sauté onion and garlic in oil in a skillet for one minute; add spinach and sauté until moisture is nearly absorbed. Blend together egg, ricotta, Parmesan and 1/2 cup mozzarella cheese; set aside. Spray an 8"x4" loaf pan with non-stick vegetable spray. Spread 1/4 cup sauce in bottom of pan; add one strip lasagna, 1/3 of spinach mixture and 1/3 of cheese mixture. Repeat layers twice; end with remaining strip lasagna, remaining 1/4 cup sauce and remaining 1/4 cup mozzarella. Cover with aluminum foil; bake at 350 degrees for 40 minutes. Uncover and bake an additional 5 minutes until golden. Let stand about 10 minutes before serving. Serves 2.

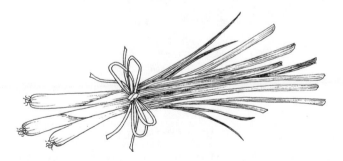

Frozen packages of chopped onion, cut-up green peppers, and stir-fry vegetables can take minutes off mealtime preparations...no chopping, mincing or dicing! It's already done for you.

Baked Penne Pasta

Melanie Lowe
Dover, DE

Add chopped black olives, mushrooms and pepperoni if you like...a very versatile recipe.

2 c. penne pasta, cooked
1 c. spaghetti sauce
1 t. dried basil
1/4 t. garlic powder

1/2 c. shredded mozzarella
   cheese, divided
1 T. grated Parmesan cheese

Stir together prepared penne, sauce, basil and garlic powder in a bowl. Spread half of mixture in a greased 2-quart casserole; top with 1/4 cup mozzarella cheese. Add remaining pasta mixture and sprinkle with remaining mozzarella and Parmesan. Bake at 350 degrees for 20 minutes or until bubbly and golden. Serves 2.

Those with families know that casseroles are a terrific choice for dinner on the run, but don't pass them over when deciding on dinner for just the 2 of you! Even with the smallest amount of leftovers in the refrigerator, the tastiest casseroles can be made.

Dinner *for* Two

Skillet Spanish Rice

Kristina Wyatt
Madera, CA

Very easy and very good!

1 c. instant rice, uncooked
1/4 c. onion, finely chopped
2 T. oil
2 c. chicken broth

1 T. taco sauce
1 t. dried cumin
1/2 t. garlic powder

Sauté rice and onion in oil; add remaining ingredients. Bring to a boil; reduce heat. Cover and simmer for 15 to 20 minutes, until rice is tender. Stir well. Serves 2.

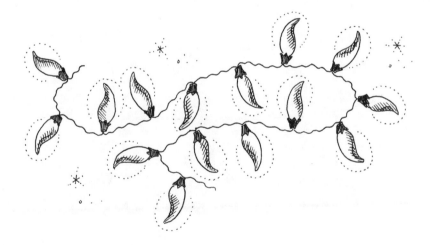

Bring a little fiesta to the table! Visit the local library and borrow some Spanish music tapes or compact disks to really set the mood during dinnertime.

Herbed Rice Pilaf

Cheri Maxwell
Gulf Breeze, FL

A simple-to-make side dish that everyone loves.

1 T. butter
1/2 c. long-cooking rice,
   uncooked
1 T. green onion, minced
1/4 t. salt
pepper to taste

1/8 t. dried tarragon
1/8 t. dried thyme
1/8 t. dried basil
1/8 t. dried parsley
1/2 c. beef broth

Melt butter in a small saucepan. Cook and stir rice and green onion until onions are translucent. Stir in seasonings; cook for one to 2 additional minutes. Add broth; bring to a boil. Simmer, covered, until rice is tender and liquid is absorbed. Serves 2.

If you've made too much rice, it's no problem. Keep it on hand for yummy rice puddings, savory casseroles, soups or stuffings.

Dinner *for* Two

Brown Sugar Beans

Marilyn Williams
Westerville, OH

A cookout favorite!

16-oz. can pork & beans
2 t. mustard
1/4 c. catsup
1/4 c. brown sugar, packed

2 t. Worcestershire sauce
1/2 c. onion, chopped
1/4 lb. ground beef, browned

Combine all ingredients and spread in a lightly oiled one-quart baking dish. Bake at 400 degrees for 20 to 30 minutes until bubbly. Serves 2.

Whether dinner is casual, served in the kitchen or a little more formal at the dining table, be sure to add simple, special touches...colorful napkins tied in a knot or perky blossoms tucked into a canning jar make mealtime more fun!

Warm Spinach & Bacon Salad

Sharon Tillman
Hampton, VA

Absolutely the best!

3 c. spinach, torn into bite-size
   pieces
1/4 c. creamy chevre cheese,
   crumbled
2 slices bacon, cut into 1/2-inch
   pieces

2 t. olive oil
1 t. balsamic vinegar
salt and pepper to taste

Arrange spinach in a salad bowl; sprinkle with cheese and set aside. Place bacon on a microwave-safe plate; microwave on high until crisp, about 2 minutes. Reserve one teaspoon drippings in a small microwave-safe bowl; drain bacon on paper towel and set aside. Whisk oil, vinegar, salt and pepper into reserved drippings. Microwave, uncovered, on high for 30 seconds, until hot. Drizzle over salad; toss to coat. Sprinkle with reserved bacon. Serves 2.

No need to follow a recipe that makes a dozen rolls...simply buy bags of frozen rolls from the grocery that let you bake only as many as needed.

✳ Dinner *for* Two

Buttery Scalloped Potatoes

Anna McMaster
Portland, OR

Creamy potatoes you'll fall in love with!

2 T. butter
2 T. all-purpose flour
1 c. milk
1/4 c. shredded Cheddar cheese
1/4 t. Worcestershire sauce

1/2 t. salt
1/8 t. pepper
2 potatoes, peeled and thinly
  sliced
Garnish: paprika

Melt butter over medium heat in a small saucepan; stir in flour until smooth. Gradually stir in milk; bring to a boil. Heat and stir for 2 minutes or until thickened. Reduce heat; stir in cheese, Worcestershire sauce, salt and pepper. Heat and stir until cheese melts. Arrange potato slices in a greased one-quart baking dish; top with cheese mixture. Cover and bake at 350 degrees for 25 minutes. Uncover and bake an additional 20 minutes, until potatoes are tender. Sprinkle with paprika. Makes 2 servings.

Float a single rose or peony bloom inside a
water-filled custard cup and center one on each
dinner plate for a romantic dinner-for-2 centerpiece.

Cheesy Baked Onions

Pamela Preston
Zanesville, OH

You'll be surprised how mellow the onions taste and how much both of you like this dish.

1 onion, sliced and separated
   into rings
1 T. butter
1 T. all-purpose flour

1/4 t. salt
1/2 c. milk
1/3 c. shredded Cheddar cheese

Arrange onions in a greased one-quart baking dish; set aside. Melt butter over low heat in a small saucepan; stir in flour and salt until smooth. Gradually stir in milk; bring to a boil. Cook and stir for 2 minutes. Remove from heat and stir in cheese until melted. Pour over onions. Bake, uncovered, at 350 degrees for 45 to 50 minutes or until onions are tender and cheese is golden. Serves 2.

Don't pass up a delicious-sounding recipe that serves 4 when you only need it to serve 2. Simply divide all quantities in half. But how to divide one egg? Here's a tip for doing just that. Beat the egg in a glass measuring cup, then spoon out half...it works!

Dinner for Two

Nutty Sweet Potatoes

Susan White
Lexington, KY

*Brown sugar, cinnamon and chopped pecans
flavor these creamy sweet potatoes.*

2 sweet potatoes, peeled and
    cubed
1/3 c. sour cream
1 T. butter, softened

1/2 t. cinnamon
1 T. milk, optional
2 T. chopped pecans
brown sugar to taste

Cover sweet potatoes with water in a saucepan. Cover pan and boil 10 to 15 minutes or until tender; drain. Mash potatoes; stir in sour cream, butter, cinnamon and enough milk for a smooth, fluffy texture. Stir in pecans; sprinkle with brown sugar to taste. Makes 2 servings.

Invite a best girlfriend over for a Sunday morning brunch...a great way for the 2 of you to spend time catching up!

Garden-Fresh Salad

Marian Buckley
Fontana, CA

A crispy, crunchy salad with a delicious garlic and herb dressing.

4 c. Romaine lettuce, torn
1/2 c. red cabbage, shredded
1/3 c. carrot, peeled and grated

1/3 c. zucchini, grated
pepper to taste
1/2 c. herb-flavored croutons

Combine lettuce, cabbage, carrots and zucchini in a bowl. Sprinkle with pepper; toss vegetables lightly to mix. Sprinkle with croutons. Toss with 1/4 to 1/3 cup Creamy Garlic Dressing to coat. Serves 2.

Creamy Garlic Dressing:

1/3 c. pine nuts
1 T. garlic, minced
1/4 t. salt
1 c. fresh parsley, packed
1-1/2 t. dried basil

1/3 c. water
3 T. cider vinegar
4 t. lemon juice
1/2 c. olive oil

Grind pine nuts in a food processor or blender for one minute until finely ground. Add garlic and salt; blend an additional 30 seconds. Add parsley and basil and pulse a few times to roughly chop. Add water, vinegar and lemon juice; blend for one minute to thoroughly combine the ingredients. Slowly drizzle in olive oil while blender is running; continue to blend an additional one minute until dressing starts to thicken. Makes 1-1/2 cups.

· Dinner *for* Two

Waldorf Salad

Rhonda Reeder
Elicott City, MD

A classic salad recipe no one should be without!

1/4 c. mayonnaise
1 T. orange juice
1 apple, cored and diced

1 stalk celery, chopped
2 T. chopped walnuts
2 leaves lettuce

Blend together mayonnaise and juice in a small bowl. Add apple, celery and walnuts; toss to coat. Arrange lettuce leaves on 2 salad plates; top with salad. Serves 2.

Whip up a pretty tablecloth in no time by using a patterned sheet. Just cut to fit the table and trim the edges with ribbon or rick-rack.

Peach Melba

Leslie Stimel
Gooseberry Patch

A fruity treat that's a snap to make.

2 peaches, peeled, pitted and
   halved
1 T. lemon juice
1 c. raspberries

1 T. extra-fine sugar
1/2 t. vanilla
1/2 c. vanilla ice cream, divided

Sprinkle peaches with lemon juice; set aside. Mash berries in a bowl; stir in sugar and vanilla. Arrange each peach half in a serving bowl. Top each with 1/4 cup of ice cream; spoon raspberry sauce over ice cream. Serves 2.

For a lighter version of Peach Melba, try substituting frozen yogurt and a sugar substitute...so easy!

∗· Dinner *for* Two

Mocha Mousse

Elizabeth Blackstone
Racine, WI

Everyone loves chocolate, and this version will be a hit!

8-oz. semi-sweet chocolate chips
3 T. powdered sugar
3 T. brewed coffee

3 egg yolks
1-1/4 c. whipping cream,
   whipped

Melt chocolate over hot water in a double boiler. Add sugar and coffee;
stir in egg yolks, one at a time. Stir until mixture thickens, remove
from heat and let cool. Add whipping cream to chocolate mixture,
blending well. Spoon into 2 serving dishes; cover and refrigerate
one hour. Serves 2.

No need to buy large, prepackaged fruits and veggies
when cooking for 2. Stop at the local farmers' market
so you can buy only what you need.

Creamy Baked Custard

Phyllis Schmatz
Kansas City, KS

A simple, old-fashioned, sweet ending to any dinner.

1 egg	3/4 t. vanilla extract
1 c. milk	1/8 t. salt
3 T. sugar	1/8 t. nutmeg

Lightly beat egg in a bowl; blend in milk, sugar, vanilla and salt. Pour into 2 ungreased 6-ounce custard cups; sprinkle with nutmeg. Set in a 9"x9" square baking pan; fill pan with water one-inch deep. Bake at 350 degrees for 35 minutes or until set. Serves 2.

After the kids are tucked in bed, pull out a favorite movie and enjoy a late-night dessert for 2. Light some candles, start a fire in the fireplace and enjoy the evening together.

Dinner *for* Two

Blueberry Cake

Sherry Gordon
Arlington Heights, IL

An old-fashioned dessert that's just as wonderful today.

1/4 c. all-purpose flour
1/4 c. sugar
1/2 t. baking powder
1/8 t. salt

1/4 c. milk
4 t. margarine, melted
1 c. blueberries

Combine flour, sugar, baking powder and salt in a small bowl; mix well. Add milk and margarine, stirring just until moistened. Spoon into 2 greased 10-ounce custard cups; top with berries. Bake at 375 degrees for 35 minutes, or until golden and berries are bubbly. Makes 2 servings.

A tin lunchbox is just the right size for a dessert made for 2. Pack dessert inside along with pint-size cartons of milk, forks and napkins. Ideal for toting to a shady spot or alongside the stream.

Raisin Bread Pudding

Virginia Watson
Scranton, PA

A true comfort dessert...yummy!

1 slice bread, cubed	3 T. water
2 T. raisins	2 T. sugar
1 egg	1/4 t. cinnamon
5-oz. can evaporated milk	1/4 t. nutmeg

Divide bread and raisins between 2 greased 8-ounce baking dishes; set aside. Beat egg, evaporated milk and water in a bowl; pour over bread. Combine sugar, cinnamon and nutmeg; sprinkle over top. Bake, uncovered, at 350 degrees for 30 to 35 minutes or until a knife inserted near center tests clean. Serve warm. Makes 2 servings.

Make desserts extra special, even if you're not baking for a crowd. Top sweet treats with dollops of whipped cream, sprinkle on powdered sugar or serve with a big scoop of ice cream or fresh berries...so yummy!

Delightful
Desserts

Keeping sweet treats on the lighter side.

✶ While "light" butters and margarines aren't meant for baking, it's easy to reduce the amount of fat in baked goodies...just substitute an equal amount of applesauce for oil.

✶ Replace the sour cream in cake recipes with plain or vanilla yogurt for a simple, lower fat version that's just as tasty.

✶ Your favorite flavor of light yogurt can be used in place of milk in any pancake recipe...they'll be so light & fluffy!

✶ Go ahead and use stick margarine if you don't have butter on hand. It's fine to swap them except in pastry recipes...margarine will create a softer dough than one made with butter.

✶ Frozen grapes make a frosty snack...much healthier than ice cream!

Delightful Desserts

Punch Bowl Cake

Georgia Medsker
Tyro, KS

l often use fat-free and sugar-free pudding and light whipped topping in this recipe...it's every bit as yummy!

18-1/4 oz. pkg. yellow cake
   mix with pudding
6-oz. box instant vanilla
   pudding mix
20-oz. can crushed pineapple,
   drained

16-oz. pkg. frozen sliced
   strawberries
4 bananas, sliced
16-oz. container frozen whipped
   topping, thawed
Garnish: chopped nuts

Prepare cake mix as package directs; let cool and cut into bite-size cubes. Prepare pudding mix according to package instructions. In a large punch bowl, layer half of each of the following: cake cubes, pudding, pineapple, strawberries, bananas, whipped topping. Repeat layers. Sprinkle with nuts. Serves 10 to 12.

Kids will giggle if you serve Punch Bowl Cake in a shiny new fish bowl!

Frosty Cherry Pie

Peggy Bidwell
Camas Valley, OR

This dessert is one we've enjoyed for 20 years...it's as fast & easy as it is delicious!

8-oz. pkg. cream cheese,
   softened
1 c. powdered sugar
1 c. whipping cream, whipped

9-inch graham cracker crust
1/2 t. almond extract
16-oz. can cherry pie filling
Optional: extra whipped cream

Blend cream cheese with an electric mixer until smooth; add powdered sugar, blending well. Slowly add whipping cream. Spoon into pie crust. Stir almond extract into pie filling and spread over cream cheese mixture. Chill one hour. Garnish with extra whipped cream, if desired. Serves 6 to 8.

For an oh-so-pretty gift, top pies with an inverted pie plate and secure both together with a bandanna.

Old-Fashioned Rice Pudding

Terri Wuensch
Hortonville, WI

This is one of those home-style desserts that's pure comfort food!

2-1/2 c. milk
1/2 c. long-cooking rice,
  uncooked

1/2 t. salt
1/4 t. sugar
1/4 t. cinnamon or nutmeg

Combine all ingredients in the top of a double boiler. Cover and cook over boiling water, stirring frequently, until rice is tender and milk is almost absorbed, for about one hour. Serves 3 to 4.

Spiff up a stack of paper napkins in a jiffy. Trim them with decorative-edge scissors, rub felt-tip markers on favorite rubber stamps and stamp away!

Nut Praline Crunch

Pamela Bures-Raybon
Edna, TX

A tin of this crunchy treat was given to me at Christmas. My family liked it so much, I asked for the recipe. Now, my sons and I make this to sell at bake sales...what a hit!

2 t. margarine	3-2/3 c. toasted oatmeal cereal
1/4 c. brown sugar, packed	squares
1/4 c. light corn syrup	1-1/4 c. bite-size crispy rice
1/4 c. baking soda	cereal squares
1/4 t. vanilla extract	2 c. mixed nuts

Combine margarine, brown sugar and corn syrup in a microwave-safe bowl. Microwave on high for one minute, or until margarine is melted. Stir in baking soda and vanilla. In a large bowl, combine cereal and nuts; gently fold in syrup mixture. Spread on an aluminum foil-lined jelly-roll pan. Bake at 250 degrees for one hour, stirring every 20 minutes. Remove from oven; place on another sheet of aluminum foil to cool. Store in an airtight container. Makes about 8 cups.

Who wouldn't love to receive an antique tin filled with sweet snacks or cookies? Tie on a handlettered tag and it's ready in no time.

Hello Dollies

Lisa Healey
Tulsa, OK

Rich and tasty, these bars make a terrific after-school treat.

2 c. vanilla wafers, crushed
1/2 c. butter, melted
1/4 c. sugar
1 c. semi-sweet chocolate chips

1 c. flaked coconut
1 c. chopped pecans
14-oz. can sweetened condensed milk

Mix first 3 ingredients and spread in the bottom of a 13"x9" baking pan. Layer with chocolate chips, coconut and pecans. Spread sweetened condensed milk over top. Bake at 325 degrees for 25 minutes. Let cool and cut into squares.
Makes 2 to 2-1/2 dozen.

A quick & easy treat...dip waffle cones into melted chocolate and sprinkle with jimmies. Set each in a glass to let chocolate harden, then fill with scoops of ice cream.

Potato Doughnuts

Lynne Davisson
Cable, OH

There's nothing like these doughnuts with a mug of spiced cider.

4 eggs, beaten
2/3 c. plus 1/2 cup sugar,
   divided
1/3 c. milk
1/3 c. shortening, melted and
   cooled
1/2 c. mashed potatoes

3-1/2 c. all-purpose flour
1 T. baking powder
3/4 t. salt
1 t. cinnamon
1/2 t. nutmeg
oil for deep frying
1 to 2 t. cinnamon

Beat eggs and 2/3 cup sugar together until light; add milk, shortening and potatoes. Set aside. Sift together dry ingredients; add to egg mixture. Refrigerate until thoroughly chilled. On a lightly floured surface, roll dough to 3/8-inch thickness; let stand 15 minutes. Cut out doughnuts using a doughnut or biscuit cutter. Heat 2 inches of oil to 375 degrees in a deep saucepan. Fry until golden; turning once. Drain on paper towels. Combine remaining sugar and cinnamon in a lunch-size paper bag. While doughnuts are still warm, place a few at a time into bag and shake to coat. Makes 3 to 4 dozen depending on size of cutter.

Stack 2 or 3 doughnuts together and wrap with ribbon, then set on individual serving plates. What a sweet treat for the kids to enjoy after raking leaves, caroling or just playing outside.

198

Creamy Raspberry Mousse

Marcia Marcoux
Charlton, MA

It's a snap to make this elegant dessert.

1-1/2 c. white chocolate chips
1 c. milk
12-oz. pkg. frozen raspberries,
 thawed
2 to 3 T. sugar
2 3.9-oz. pkgs. white chocolate
 instant pudding mix

2 c. frozen whipped topping,
 thawed
Garnish: 1/2 c. chopped
 pistachios

Heat chocolate chips and milk in microwave on high setting for 15 seconds at a time, stirring between each interval, until chips are melted. Place in refrigerator until cold; stir occasionally to minimize separation. Process raspberries and sugar in blender until smooth. Strain seeds, if desired; set aside. When chocolate mixture is cold, add pudding mix; beat for about 2 minutes. Fold in whipped topping; refrigerate for at least one hour. Divide into 6 individual serving bowls; top each with about 2 tablespoons of raspberry mixture. Sprinkle with pistachios if desired. Makes 6 servings.

Spoon individual servings of mousse into tall plastic goblets...a fun way to celebrate family night!

California Peach Pie

Mary Hageny
Rhinelander, WI

Fresh peaches make this pie a real winner!

3 c. peaches, pitted, peeled and
   sliced
9-inch pie crust
2 eggs, beaten

1 c. milk
1 c. sugar
cinnamon to taste

Arrange peaches in pie crust so that the entire crust is covered. In a bowl, combine eggs, milk and sugar. Mix together thoroughly and pour over peaches. Sprinkle cinnamon on top. Bake at 425 degrees for 20 minutes; reduce oven to 350 degrees and bake for an additional 15 to 20 minutes. Serves 6 to 8.

Clever placecards in a snap! Just use a permanent marker to write guests' names on helium-filled balloons and tie to each chair.

French Apple Crisp

Linda Day
Wall, NJ

French Apple Crisp is always a favorite because it reminds me of my mother-in-law, who passed the recipe along to me.

1/2 c. butter, divided
4 c. apples, cored, peeled and
   sliced
1/4 c. rum or apple juice
2/3 c. sugar, divided
1/8 t. cinnamon
1/2 c. blanched almonds, finely
   chopped

1/2 c. all-purpose flour
1/8 t. salt
1/2 t. vanilla extract
Garnish: vanilla ice cream or
   whipped cream

Melt 1/4 cup butter in a large skillet. Sauté apples in butter until tender, about 5 minutes. Remove from heat: pour rum or apple juice over apples. Stir in 1/3 cup sugar and cinnamon. Let stand for 30 minutes. Measure almonds, flour, remaining sugar and salt into a bowl. Cut in remaining butter with pastry blender or 2 knives until mixture resembles coarse meal. Add vanilla. Evenly spread apple mixture in a greased 2-quart baking dish. Sprinkle half of the pastry mixture over the apples. Bake at 400 degrees for 15 minutes. Sprinkle remaining pastry mixture on top. Bake an additional 15 minutes or until golden. Serve warm with vanilla ice cream or whipped cream if desired. Serves 10 to 12.

Make those you meet feel like an angel has kissed them, and leave behind gentle memories when you go.

-Lynn Ray

Warm Cinnamon Peaches

Jimi Paderick
Seven Springs, NC

*This is one of those recipes I know I can count on for a light
dessert, and it's a quick fix for company.*

29-oz. can peach halves, drained   2 to 3 T. cinnamon
1/2 c. sugar

Arrange peaches in a microwave-safe dish with cut side up. Sprinkle
sugar and cinnamon over peaches. Heat in microwave on high setting
for 5 to 7 minutes. Serve warm. Makes 8 to 10 servings.

World's Greatest Fruit Crumble

Amy Puckett
Allen, TX

With only 2 ingredients, this is an incredible time-saver!

21-oz. can pie filling   18-1/4 oz. pkg. yellow cake mix

Spray a 13"x9" glass pan with non-stick cooking spray. Pour in pie
filling. Sprinkle the cake mix on top. Bake at 350 degrees for
30 minutes or until bubbling and golden brown on top. Serves 8 to 10.

*Corral a cookbook collection in
style! Spruce up an old
dresser drawer with a coat of
latex paint and some new
hardware. Now family
favorites will be at your
fingertips when needed.*

Chocolatey Chocolate Cake

Margaret Clark
Rockford, IL

Add some chocolate curls for even more chocolatey taste!

3 c. all-purpose flour	2 c. sugar
6 T. baking cocoa	2 t. baking soda
1 t. salt	3/4 c. oil
2 T. vinegar	2 t. vanilla extract
2 c. water	Garnish: 12-oz. can frosting

Combine all ingredients; mix well and spread in a 13"x9" greased and floured pan. Bake for 30 minutes at 350 degrees. Frost with your favorite chocolate or peanut butter frosting. Makes 8 to 10 servings.

A centerpiece in a snap...fill dainty egg cups with water and a perky blossom.

Tutti-Frutti Dessert

Wendy Lee Paffenroth
Pine Island, NY

Swap out the orange-flavored gelatin for strawberry and add sliced frozen strawberries for a whole new flavor.

8-oz. can crushed pineapple,
   drained and juice reserved
11-oz. can mandarin oranges,
   drained and juice reserved

2 c. boiling water
1-3/4 c. dairy topping
6-oz. pkg. orange gelatin mix
1-1/2 c. mini marshmallows

Place pineapple and oranges in large bowl. Add cold water to reserved fruit juices to equal one cup of liquid; set aside. Mix gelatin in boiling water and stir until dissolved; refrigerate until it starts to set, about one hour. When gelatin is thickened, mix with whipped topping, fruit and juices. Whisk until well blended; add marshmallows and pour into a serving bowl. Refrigerate about 3 hours or until firm. Serves 6 to 8.

Keeps grocery lists and refrigerator artwork hanging in style! Use hot glue to attach magnets to game pieces...dominoes and checkers are fun.

Delightful Desserts

Crustless Coconut Pie

Glenda Geohagen
DeFuniak Springs, FL

*The ultimate dessert when you discover
you don't have a pie crust on hand!*

4 eggs	1/2 c. self-rising flour
1-3/4 c. sugar	1 c. flaked coconut
2 c. milk	1 t. vanilla extract
1/4 c. butter	

Beat eggs until frothy. Add other ingredients in order given; mix well. Spread in 2, 9" pie plates; bake at 350 degrees for 25 to 30 minutes until golden. Makes 6 to 12 servings.

*For a quick dessert garnish, chop nuts and toast them
in a shallow baking pan at 350 degrees for
5 to 10 minutes. Cool, then place in plastic bags and
freeze. Ready to sprinkle on pies, cakes or ice cream
whenever you need them.*

Easy Peanut Butter Dessert

Phyllis Peters
Three Rivers, MI

Just keep it in the freezer until you find you need a quick dessert.

2 c. milk
1 c. creamy peanut butter
3.4-oz. pkg. instant vanilla
    pudding mix

1 c. sour cream
9-inch graham cracker crust

Combine milk, peanut butter, pudding mix and sour cream; mix well. Spread in pie crust and freeze until firm. Serves 6 to 8.

Peanut Butter Balls

Sarah Anglin
Doniphan, MO

Drizzle with melted chocolate for a chocolatey version.

1 c. peanut butter
1/2 c. honey

1/2 c. instant powdered milk
Optional: 1/4 c. raisins

Mix ingredients thoroughly, adding raisins if desired. Roll into one-inch balls. Place on wax paper-lined baking sheet. Chill in refrigerator until set. Makes about 3 dozen.

Save time...there's no need to sift all-purpose flour, instead sift only cake flour because it has a tendency to pack.

Delightful Desserts

Berry Easy Cobbler

Sheila Taggiano
Castaic, CA

Use any favorite fruit...you can't go wrong!

1-1/4 c. all-purpose flour
1/2 c. plus 1/3 c. sugar, divided
1-1/2 t. baking powder
3/4 c. milk

1/3 c. butter, melted
3 c. blueberries
Garnish: vanilla ice cream or
    whipped cream

Combine flour, 1/2 cup sugar and baking powder in a medium mixing bowl. Add milk and butter; stir until just combined. Spread in a greased 8"x8" baking dish. Sprinkle evenly with blueberries, then with remaining sugar. Bake at 350 degrees for 40 to 45 minutes or until a toothpick inserted in the center comes out clean. Serve warm with vanilla ice cream or whipped cream. Makes 4 to 6 servings.

A simple way to remember Sunday dinner at Grandma's house...use a vintage hankie as a mat for her handwritten recipe cards. What a sweet remembrance.

Sweet Decadence

Jo Neddo
Whitehall, NY

*Chocolate pudding, pecans, whipped cream...what other
name could this dessert have?*

1 c. all-purpose flour
1/2 c. butter, softened
1/4 c. brown sugar, packed
1/4 c. chopped pecans
2 pts. vanilla ice cream, softened
3.4-oz. box instant vanilla
    pudding mix

3.4-oz. box instant chocolate
    pudding mix
2 c. milk
16-oz. container frozen whipped
    topping, thawed
Garnish: shaved chocolate bar

Combine flour, butter, sugar and pecans; spread on a baking sheet.
Bake at 350 degrees for 15 minutes; crumble into a 13"x9" baking pan
and set aside. Mix together ice cream, puddings and milk; spread over
baked crust. Top with whipped topping; sprinkle with chocolate
shavings. Refrigerate until firm. Serves 6 to 8.

Consider having a once-a-year Pie Night! Friends &
family bring their favorite pie to share, and everyone
helps out with the dishes!

Delightful Desserts

Sugarless Cake

Jan Ramsey
Wellington, TX

*A terrific cake recipe for those watching their sugar intake,
or if you just want a moist cake everyone will love.*

2 eggs, beaten
32-oz. can applesauce
2 c. all-purpose flour
1 t. baking soda
1 t. baking powder
2-1/2 T. liquid calorie-free
   sweetener

1 t. ground cloves
1 t. allspice
1 t. vanilla extract
1 c. butter, softened
8-oz. box chopped dates
1 c. chopped pecans

Combine all ingredients in order given. Mix well; spread in a greased and floured Bundt® pan. Bake at 350 degrees for one hour. Serves 10 to 12.

Serve a couple cookies or a plump brownie with a big bowl of ice cream...a "dressed-up" dessert with very little effort.

Strawberry Pizza

Micki Stephens
Marion, OH

*Top with some kiwi or banana slices or
even chocolate curls if you'd like.*

18-oz. tube refrigerated
    sugar cookie dough
8-oz. pkg. cream cheese,
    softened
2 c. frozen whipped topping,
    thawed

1 t. vanilla extract
1 c. powdered sugar
14-oz. pkg. strawberry glaze
16-oz. pkg. strawberries, hulled
    and sliced

Roll out dough on a greased 12" pizza pan; bake according to package
directions. Set aside. Mix cream cheese, whipped topping, vanilla and
powdered sugar together; spread over cooled crust. Top with glaze and
strawberries. Serves 6 to 8.

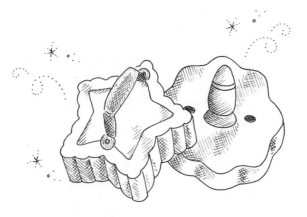

Just for fun, sprinkle edible glitter on sugary treats!

1-2-3 Cake

Carole Barbaro
Clayton, NJ

What can I say...it's as easy as 1-2-3!

20-oz. can crushed pineapple
21-oz. can cherry pie filling
18-1/2 oz. yellow cake mix,
    divided

1 c. chopped walnuts
1 c. margarine, sliced

Place pineapple with juice in an ungreased 13"x9" baking dish; spread pie filling evenly over the top. Sprinkle with half of the cake mix, then with nuts. Sprinkle with remaining cake mix; dot margarine over top. Bake at 350 degrees for one hour. Serves 8 to 10.

Forget about anything fussy...enjoy dessert outside and let the crumbs fall where they may!

Peanut Butter Bars

Kris Warner
Circleville, OH

Perfect for tucking into lunchboxes.

1/2 c. butter, softened
1/2 c. sugar
1/2 c. brown sugar, packed
1/2 c. creamy peanut butter
1 egg, beaten
1 t. vanilla extract
1 c. all-purpose flour

1/2 c. quick-cooking oats,
  uncooked
1 t. baking soda
1/4 t. salt
1/2 c. semi-sweet chocolate
  chips

In a bowl, blend together butter, sugars and peanut butter; add egg and vanilla. Mix well; set aside. Mix flour, oats, baking soda and salt; stir into butter mixture. Spread in a greased 13"x9" baking pan; sprinkle with chocolate chips. Bake at 350 degrees for 20 to 25 minutes; cool for 10 minutes. Spread frosting over top; cut into bars. Makes 3 to 4 dozen.

Frosting:

2 c. powdered sugar
2 T. creamy peanut butter

2 T. milk

Mix all ingredients together until smooth.

Delightful Desserts

Old Dominion Chess Pie

Carol Hickman
Kingsport, TN

Think of it as chocolate pecan pie...yum!

5 T. baking cocoa
1-1/2 c. sugar
2 eggs, beaten
1/2 c. chopped pecans

1/4 c. butter, melted
1/2 c. evaporated milk
1/2 c. flaked coconut
9-inch pie crust, unbaked

Mix the first 7 ingredients together; pour into pie crust. Bake at 400 degrees for 30 minutes. Let cool completely. Serves 6 to 8.

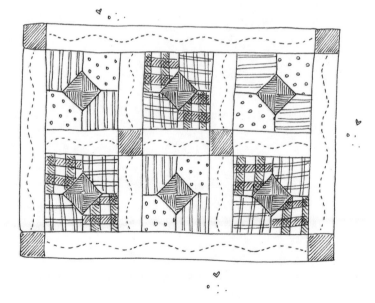

For a new spin, serve glasses of icy milk from pint-size canning jars.

Fudge-Brownie Pie

Flo Burtnett
Gage, OK

This recipe first appeared in a 1914 cookbook published by the YMCA and it's as good now as it was then.

1 c. sugar
1/2 c. margarine, melted
2 eggs
1/2 c. all-purpose flour

1/3 c. baking cocoa
1/4 t. salt
1 t. vanilla extract
1/2 c. chopped pecans

In a mixing bowl, beat sugar and margarine. Add eggs; mix well. Stir in flour, cocoa and salt; mix in vanilla and pecans. Pour into a greased and floured 9" pie plate; bake at 350 degrees for 25 to 30 minutes. Serves 6.

If friends are dropping by for dessert, mix & match the tablecloths, napkins, cups & saucers...a fuss-free way to set the table.

Delightful Desserts

Turtle Cake

Laura Strausberger
Cary, IL

This recipe came from my friend, Andrea. Since we first met, we've both moved often, but have still managed to keep in touch. It's a great cake that always makes me think of her.

18-1/2 oz. German chocolate
   cake mix
14-oz. caramels, unwrapped
1/2 c. evaporated milk

1/2 c. margarine
1 c. chopped walnuts
1 c. semi-sweet chocolate chips

Prepare cake according to package directions; pour half of the batter into a greased and floured 13"x9" baking pan. Bake at 350 degrees for 15 minutes. Melt caramels, milk and margarine in a saucepan; blend well and spread over baked cake. Sprinkle with walnuts and chocolate chips; pour remaining batter over top. Bake for an additional 20 minutes; cool. Serves 8 to 12.

Grease and flour cake pans in one easy step. Combine 1/2 cup shortening with 1/4 cup all-purpose flour. Keep this handy mix in a covered container at room temperature.

Nutty Pudding Cake

Sandy Jacobson
Maxwell, IA

I have also made this cake substituting pecans for the almonds and chocolate chips for the butterscotch...both versions are very good.

18-1/2 oz. yellow cake mix
15-3/4 oz. can butterscotch
   pudding
2 eggs

1/3 c. sugar
6-oz. pkg. butterscotch chips
1 c. sliced almonds

Blend together cake mix, pudding and eggs; spread in a greased and floured 13"x9" baking pan. Top with sugar, butterscotch chips and almonds; bake at 375 degrees for 30 minutes. Serves 8 to 12.

Finding out at the last minute you're in charge of treats for the after-school get-together? Just fill a market basket with fresh fruit and fruit dip for a yummy and healthy treat.

Cookies & Cream Dessert

Jodi Wieland
Templeton, IA

Cookies, pudding and whipped cream...no one can resist this!

20-oz. pkg. chocolate sandwich
  cookies, crushed
1/2 c. margarine, melted
2 3.4-oz. pkgs. instant vanilla
  pudding mix

3 c. milk
8-oz. pkg. cream cheese,
  softened
8-oz. container frozen whipped
  topping, thawed

Mix cookie crumbs with margarine; reserve one cup of mixture. Press remaining mixture in the bottom of a 13"x9" baking pan; set aside. Combine pudding mix, milk, cream cheese and whipped topping; spread over cookie mixture. Sprinkle with reserved cookie mixture; refrigerate for one hour. Serves 15.

Freeze dollops of whipped cream ahead of time to use for desserts...it's easy. Just drop heaping tablespoonfuls onto a chilled baking sheet and freeze. Remove from the baking sheet and store in a plastic zipping bag. To use, place a dollop on dessert servings and let stand a few minutes.

Almond Grahams

Patricia MacLean
Ontario, Canada

*If you want larger servings (and you will!)
simply serve them cut into squares.*

12 whole graham crackers
1/2 c. butter

1 c. brown sugar, packed
1 c. sliced almonds

Place crackers in a greased 15"x10" jelly-roll pan; set aside. Bring butter and brown sugar to a boil in a saucepan; stir constantly for 2 to 3 minutes until sugar melts. Pour over crackers, spreading evenly. Sprinkle with sliced almonds. Bake at 400 degrees for 5 minutes; break or cut into pieces. Makes 8 cups.

How clever! Serve bars or cookies in a whimsical bottle-cap bowl. Paint a wooden bowl with acrylic paint and let dry. Seal the paint with a protective finish. Turn the bowl upside-down and apply hot glue to the bottom edges of a bottle cap. Press in place and hold until secure. Repeat with as many bottle caps as you'd like to add.

Sweet & Simple Comfort Cake

Carolynn Smith
Roseville, CA

*A fruity, brown-sugar topped cake...try a slice with
a cup of herbal tea.*

1 c. sugar
1 c. all-purpose flour
1 t. baking soda
1/8 t. salt
15-oz. can fruit cocktail, drained

1 egg, beaten
3/4 c. brown sugar, packed
1/2 c. chopped nuts
Garnish: whipped cream

Sift sugar, flour, baking soda and salt together; stir in fruit cocktail and egg. Mix well; pour into a 13"x9" baking pan. Sprinkle with brown sugar and nuts; bake at 350 degrees for 45 minutes. Let cool; top with whipped cream. Serves 8 to 10.

Good china and candles aren't just for the holidays or special celebrations...use them to brighten everyday meals!

Index

Index

Marinades & Sauces

Index

We've cooked up a whole collection of Gooseberry Patch® books!

Have a taste for more? Call us toll-free at

1-800-854-6673

We'll send you our latest catalog filled with kitchenware, candles, handmade quilts, gourmet goodies, enamelware, bowls, bubble night lights and our very own line of cookbooks, calendars and organizers!

Phone us:
1·800·854·6673

Fax us:
1·740·363·7225

Visit our website.
www.gooseberrypatch.com

Send us your favorite recipe...

and the memory that makes it special for you! If we select your recipe for a brand new **Gooseberry Patch** cookbook, your name will appear right along with it...and you'll receive a FREE copy of the book! Mail to:

Vickie & Jo Ann
Gooseberry Patch, Dept. Book
600 London Road
Delaware, Ohio 43015

*Please include the number of servings and all other necessary information!

quick & easy ✏ no-fuss fare ☆ all time favorites: here's the scoop ● easy as 1·2·3 ◐ oh-so simple: come on in! cookin' up fun! fix it fast ● no-fuss fare ● easy, breezy ☆ quick & easy! ready in no time ● all time favorites ● cookin' up fun! fix it fast ● easy, breezy